# The *Church* of the
# OPEN Door

The *Church* of the
# OPEN Door
## Ministry Dynamics Then and Now

## WARREN W. WIERSBE

CLC
PUBLICATIONS

The Church of the Open Door
*Published by CLC Publications*

*U.S.A.*
P.O. Box 1449, Fort Washington, PA 19034

*GREAT BRITAIN*
51 The Dean, Alresford, Hants. SO24 9BJ

*NEW ZEALAND*
118 King Street, Palmerston North 4410

Printed in the United States of America
ISBN-10 (trade paper): 1-61958-010-1
ISBN-13 (trade paper): 978-1-61958-010-7

Unless otherwise noted, all Scripture quotations are from *Today's New International Version*, Copyright 2001, 2005 by International Bible Society and published by Zondervan.

Scripture quotations marked NASB are from the New American Standard Bible®, © 1960, 1962, 1963, 1968, 1971, 1972, 1973, 1975, 1977, 1995 by The Lockman Foundation.
Used by permission.

Scripture quotations marked KJV are from the Holy Bible, King James Version.

Italics in Scripture quotations are the emphasis of the author.

# Contents

1.  The Church of the Closed Door ..................................7

2.  The Church of the Open Door ............................. 13

3.  The Church of the Almost Closed Door .............. 25

4.  The Ephesian Emphasis, Part 1............................. 45

5.  The Ephesian Emphasis, Part 2............................. 59

6.  The Ephesian Emphasis, Part 3............................. 87

7.  Listening to the Holy Spirit.................................... 99

    Endnotes................................................................ 115

# 1

## The Church of the Closed Door

THE HISTORY of the church of Jesus Christ is the record of the conflict between open doors and closed minds.

Whenever the Lord opened a door, people with closed minds tried to shut it, and too often they succeeded. Then the Lord would raise up men and women of faith who prayed the doors open again and went through them to defeat the Enemy and build the church.

Let's go back to the beginning of the church as recorded in the first chapters of the Book of Acts. The time in Acts 1 is forty days after our Lord's resurrection and the place is a large upper room in the city of Jerusalem where one hundred and twenty men and women have gathered to wait and pray. These people will play a very important role in what God is about to do, for in their hearts they treasured the only message that could change the world and solve its problems—the good news of salvation through faith in Jesus Christ.

Jesus had been crucified and buried and on the third day raised from the dead. It was fifty days from His resurrection until Pentecost, and during the forty days after His resurrection, He had been seen alive by one witness after another, including five hundred people at one time (1 Cor. 15:6). There was no question that Jesus was alive. Before His ascension Jesus had prepared His disciples to carry the message of salvation to the whole world, starting in Jerusalem and eventually reaching the Gentile world.

---

*If that message was so important, why were these dedicated followers of Jesus Christ behind closed doors? Why not leave the upper room and spread this wonderful message.*

---

But if that message was so important, why were these dedicated followers of Jesus Christ behind closed doors? Why not leave the upper room and spread this wonderful message to the people in Jerusalem who so desperately needed it? *Because the believers were not yet equipped for service.* They needed "a change of clothes."

"I am going to send you what my Father has promised," Jesus told them before His ascension, "but stay in the city until you have been clothed with power from on high" (Luke 28:49). The power of the Holy Spirit was the spiritual equipping they needed to glorify Christ and win the lost. We need to be "clothed" with that same power today, and we can be if we set aside the substitutes that have robbed the church of power and Jesus of glory.

At the onset of a new era in salvation history, the Lord often commanded His servants to go apart and invest time in prayer and spiritual preparation. Moses spent forty years caring for sheep in Midian before he confronted Pharaoh in Egypt and led the exodus. Before ascending the throne of Israel, David had perhaps seven to ten years of exile in the wilderness, fleeing from King Saul, and those were years of preparation for leadership. God told the prophet Elijah to hide himself for three years before He sent him to deal with wicked King Ahab, and the apostle Paul spent three years in Arabia after his conversion before launching into his ministry. Even our Lord Jesus after His baptism spent forty days alone in the wilderness. First the preparation, then the power.

If we don't wait upon the Lord and allow Him to equip us, we will not be successful in our work for the Lord. We're not prepared to share His gospel until we are "clothed" with divine power. "But you will receive power when the Holy Spirit comes on you," Jesus had promised, "and you will be my witnesses in Jerusalem, and in all Judea and Samaria, and to the ends of the earth" (Acts 1:8). Open doors! No matter what we may have in the way of talent, experience, wealth or training, if we don't have the Holy Spirit's fullness, we don't have anything and we aren't ready to serve.

When I was a young pastor, I heard A.W. Tozer say, "If God were to take the Holy Spirit out of this world, most of what the church is doing would go right on and nobody would know the difference."

Ouch! Who had told him about my ministry?

Years later, I read in one of his printed sermons, "Now, a plain word here about the Christian church trying to carry on in its own power. That kind of Christianity makes God sick, for it is trying to run a heavenly institution after an earthly manner."[1] What many churches are today, Dr. Tozer described years ago, and he was right.

The door to the upper room was closed, not because the believers were afraid that an enemy might come in, but *because they knew that they themselves were unprepared to go out and witness to a lost world.* The gospel of Jesus Christ is "the power of God that brings salvation" (Rom. 1:16), but powerless witnesses can't successfully proclaim this powerful gospel. "[Our] gospel came to you not simply with words but also with power, with the Holy Spirit and deep conviction" (1 Thess. 1:5). Powerless witnesses are speechless and fruitless witnesses.

But weren't those believers in the upper room already adequately equipped to go out and witness for Jesus? After all, they had known Christ personally, and some were even related to Him on the human level. The apostles had walked with Him daily and had listened to Him teach. They had heard Him pray, and He had taught them to pray. They had performed miracles and had even experienced miracles. (Peter walked on the water.) They believed in each other and were united in prayer, and they sought the will of God in the Scriptures as they appointed a new apostle to replace Judas. Jesus had opened His disciples' minds to understand the Scriptures (Luke 24:45), so what more was needed?

The one thing they lacked was the power of the Holy Spirit for their witness and ministry. Jesus said, "Apart from me you can do nothing" (John 15:5). The Holy Spirit came on the Day of Pentecost and gave the believers the power to witness, and because of that witness three thousand people trusted Jesus Christ and entered the family of God. These new believers were baptized, became a part of the church fellowship and went out to witness to others.

In the book of Acts, Dr. Luke tells us how the early church won thousands to Christ in Jerusalem, reaped a harvest in Judea and Samaria, and then launched out into the Gentile world where they planted churches throughout the Roman Empire. It was the power of the Holy Spirit in the lives of ordinary people that accomplished this extraordinary ministry.

Those courageous first-century Christians had none of the "evangelical luxuries" that our churches possess today. They owned no buildings but met outdoors, in the temple courts or the synagogues, and in private homes ("house churches"). They had no big budgets (Acts 3:6), boasted of no political clout, graduated from no religious schools (Acts 4:13) and engaged in no slick advertising campaigns. It's also worth noting that they had none of the modern technology that is so evident in churches today. But in spite of these "deficiencies," they carried the gospel from Jerusalem to Rome and beyond. How did they do it? They depended on the power of the Holy Spirit.

---

*The Holy Spirit doesn't work in an isolated vacuum.*

---

It comes as a shock to many Christians to learn that the Holy Spirit doesn't work in an isolated vacuum. Too many believers imagine that the Spirit moves around like a mysterious invisible cloud and touches hearts here and there, but that's not the way He works. *The Holy Spirit works in and through God's people as they pray, share God's Word and seek to glorify God's Son.* The Spirit's "tools" are dedicated people, the Word of God and prayer. "He [the Holy Spirit] will glorify me," said Jesus (John 16:14). If anyone other than Jesus Christ is being glorified in our churches, then the Holy Spirit is not at work and will not bless. "I am the Lord; that is my name! I will not yield my glory to another or my praise to idols" (Isa. 42:8). How tragic it is to see Christians today exalting preachers, musicians, religious celebrities and even well-known unconverted people, but failing to give glory to Jesus Christ, the only one who really deserves it.

What would happen to our churches today if church leaders had the courage to do what those first believers did: clear the schedule and devote ten days to uninterrupted praise and prayer?

We might experience some of what Dr. Luke described in Acts chapter 2.

## *Ministry Principles from Acts 1*

1. God's people must learn to wait on the Lord, in unity and faith. Without spiritual preparation there can be no blessing.

2. As we wait, we must pray and believe God's promise of power.

3. We must search the Word and seek the leading of the Holy Spirit.

4. Once we know God's will, we must obey it.

5. God has a plan for each local church and we must follow it. "Therefore, my dear friends . . . continue to work out your own salvation with fear and trembling, for it is God who works in you to will and to act in order to fulfill his good purpose" (Phil. 2:12–13).

# 2

# The Church of the Open Door

IN THE FIRST two chapters of his Gospel record, Dr. Luke describes how Jesus was born into this world in a human body through the power of the Holy Spirit. "The Word became flesh and made his dwelling among us" (John 1:14). We call this miracle the Incarnation. In the first two chapters of the Book of Acts, Dr. Luke explains how the *spiritual* body of Christ—the church—was born into this world on the Day of Pentecost.

When the Holy Spirit came in power from heaven and baptized the believers, this united them to one another and to the exalted Head of the church in heaven (Acts 1:7; 1 Cor. 12:12–14). The Spirit also filled the believers with power for witnessing (Acts 1:8; 2:4) and led them out of the upper room. They were no longer "the church of the closed door." The Spirit enabled them publicly to worship the Lord (Acts 2:11) and to bear witness that Jesus of Nazareth was alive and ready to save all who would call upon Him (Acts 2:14–41). As a result, about three thousand people were converted and became a part of the church. A few days later, two thousand more trusted Christ (Acts 3:4).

Throughout the Book of Acts, Dr. Luke describes how the church expanded both numerically and geographically (2:41, 47; 4:4; 5:14; 6:1, 7; 9:31; 11:24; 12:24; 16:5; 19:20). Now that they were "the church of the opened door" and empowered by the Holy Spirit, they could effectively declare the good news of Jesus Christ to others. The Lord is willing to open doors for us today if only we will take time to pray, feed on the Word and receive the enabling power of the Spirit. Neither the gospel nor the Spirit has changed, but the church has changed and is trying to get along without a message and the power to share it.

---

*The Lord is willing to open doors for us today if only we will take time to pray, feed on the Word and receive the enabling power of the Spirit.*

---

The early believers didn't open the door of the upper room and ask the outsiders to come in, nor did they put a sign on the door that read "Everybody Welcome!" *The believers left the upper room and went out to witness personally to the people in Jerusalem.*[2] In Peter's congregation that day were Jews "from every nation under heaven" (Acts 2:5) who had come to celebrate the feast (Acts 2:8–11). This was the beginning of the church's witness "to the ends of the earth" (Acts 1:8). The Feast of Pentecost was primarily dedicated to giving thanks for the harvest, but Jewish people also used that day to celebrate the giving of the law to Israel. But the Pentecost described in Acts 2 focused not on law but on the grace of God, and it led to a joyful harvest of precious souls.

There is a pattern in the way God works in the lives of His children. First, we trust Jesus Christ and experience God's gracious salvation, witnessed and sealed by the Spirit (Eph. 1:13–14). Then we publicly identify with God's people and join them in praying, worshiping, serving and witnessing. By faith we receive the

Spirit's power and share God's love and truth with those who are lost. This has always been the biblical pattern for the church's ministry. Jesus needed a body in order to accomplish His salvation work on earth, and today He needs a body to carry His message to others. That body is the church collectively (Eph. 1:22–23) and the individual believer yielded to Him (Rom. 12:1–2).

God's method for ministry is *incarnation*, not imitation. If some current church leaders had been in charge at Pentecost, they would have taken a survey, chosen a target audience, thought up a clever slogan and determined a novel way to communicate their message. While communication techniques and technology certainly have their place in Christian witness, they are never substitutes for Spirit-filled believers exalting Jesus Christ and declaring His gospel. Technology and techniques are fruitless without God's blessing. Imitation means we are cheap copies, but incarnation means that the Holy Spirit is enabling us to be effective originals. If we are imitators at all, we imitate Christ and the godly people who follow Him (1 Cor. 11:1).

"Therefore, my dear friends . . . continue to work out your salvation with fear and trembling, for it is God who works in you to will and to act in order to fulfill his good purpose" (Phil. 2:12–13). Although these words apply to each of us personally, they were originally written to the Christian congregation at Philippi. They describe incarnation, the Spirit working in and through believers and glorifying Jesus Christ. "The church is not a company of people who copy or borrow from one another," wrote Watchman Nee, commenting on Matthew 16:17, "but those who, like Peter, have firsthand experience of the Father in heaven."[3]

In a powerful sermon on "freshness," Charles Haddon Spurgeon said,

Christian people can lose the freshness of their own selves by
imitating one another. . . . Drop into one particular groove,
and run in it; take up one line of things, and stick to it; and
you will very soon find yourself as far from freshness as a bit
of leather which has been worked on an engine to revolve
forever and ever in the same course. The beauty of real life lies
much in its variety.[4]

Freshness and variety are products of creativity and must not
be confused with novelty and trendiness. The believer is a new
creation in Christ (2 Cor. 5:17) and is "like the owner of a house
who brings out of his storeroom new treasures as well as old"
(Matt. 13:52). Our clocks need both the minute hand and the
hour hand to record the time accurately, and the church needs
both the old and the new to minister to the times effectively.
When I was serving in Youth for Christ years ago, our slogan
was, "Geared to the times, anchored to the Rock." I recommend
it to you. The Holy Spirit is infinitely creative. It's Satan who is
the imitator.

People who call themselves "conservatives" but who resist
creative changes that can bring improvement aren't conservatives at all; they are *preservatives*. During my years of pastoral
ministry, I was often called to be a bridge builder, strengthen-
ing the old and moving into the new. I borrowed my approach
from philosopher Alfred North Whitehead: order in the midst
of change and change in the midst of order. Change without order produces chaos and anarchy, but order without change leads
to stagnation and paralysis. Anarchy and chaos are exciting but
dangerous; cemeteries and museums can be depressing.

As we study Acts 2, we need to focus on the essentials and
not be detoured by the accidentals. Pentecost with its special
signs will not be repeated any more than the crucifixion and resurrection of our Lord will be repeated. However, there are three

occurrences at Pentecost that can help us better understand what it means to be part of an "open door" church: the sound like a rushing wind, the tongues like fire and the accusation from the crowd that the believers were drunk (Acts 2:2–3, 13).

The sound like a rushing wind was what drew the crowd together. They didn't feel the wind; they heard it. It began in the upper room and then accompanied the believers as they moved out, probably to the temple where Peter addressed the crowd. Wind is an essential part of the world of nature that God created. According to meteorologists, if the wind stopped blowing, everything would eventually die; so when we think of the wind, we think of life, power and refreshment.

In Scripture the wind is one of many symbols of the Holy Spirit who, like the wind, is invisible, powerful and mysterious (John 3:8). The Spirit is the "breath of life" to us, just as He is the water of life (John 7:37–39), and Jesus is the bread of life (John 6:35) and the light of life (John 8:12). Without light, air, food and water, we couldn't survive.

What appeared above the believers' heads was not literal fire but "what seemed to be tongues of fire" (Acts 2:3). Fire speaks not only of judgment but also of power and purity, and fire can be either a servant or a destroyer. It can cook the food or burn down the house; it all depends on what we do. *When you combine fire and a rushing wind, you have a blaze!*

The church was about to declare a message that would "spread like wildfire" and alter the course of human history. Our tongues can be ignited by heaven, as were the believers' tongues at Pentecost, and we can share the message of life, or our tongues can be ignited by hell (James 3:6) and bring destruction. "The tongue has the power of life and death" (Prov. 18:21).

The third image in Acts 2 is that of wine (Acts 2:13). The skeptics in the crowd accused the believers of being drunk, a charge with Peter was easily able to refute. In Ephesians 5:18–21 Paul used wine to symbolize the Holy Spirit, and he contrasted the fullness of the Spirit with drunkenness. People who are drunk are out of control, while the fruit of the Spirit is self-control (Gal. 5:23). Drunks feel and act very brave, and are quite noisy about it, but no matter how they boast, they are deceiving themselves because they are actually weak. Spirit-filled (Spirit-controlled) Christians have boldness in the Lord because they experience His power within. The "joy" of drunkards is artificial and leaves them in worse shape, while the joy of the Lord is the strength of believers (Neh. 8:10) and helps them better serve their Master.

When the believers left the upper room and began to worship God publicly in foreign languages, the crowds were utterly amazed. "Aren't all these who are speaking Galileans?" the visitors asked; ". . . we hear them declaring the wonders of God in our own tongues" (Acts 2:7, 11). "Galilee of the Gentiles" (Matt. 4:16) was not considered a prestigious place to live. When Philip told Nathanael that Jesus came from Nazareth in Galilee, Nathanael replied, "Nazareth! Can anything good come from there?" (John 1:46). But empowered by the Holy Spirit, the Galilean believers glorified God in their worship and prepared the crowd to hear Peter's sermon, believe in Jesus and be saved.

---

*A truly Spirit-filled church will have three outstanding characteristics: it is unified, magnified and multiplied.*

---

The church of the open door is definitely a witnessing church that is neither isolated nor insulated from lost people. As with Jesus, so with the church: incarnation leads to identification. The church identifies with those who need Christ and it shares the Word with them. But when the preaching is ended and the new believers have been integrated into the fellowship, a truly Spirit-filled church will have three outstanding characteristics: it is unified, magnified and multiplied. (Read carefully Acts 2:42–47.)

Let's begin with *unified*. "All the believers were together and had everything in common" (Acts 2:44). The one hundred and twenty believers had been together in the upper room during their ten days of prayer (Acts 1:14), which meant much more than occupying the same room. They were one in heart, mind and will, and this kind of unity continued after three thousand new Christians were added to the church. The original nucleus of one hundred and twenty believers was now outnumbered by the new believers, but that didn't create any problems because God's Spirit was controlling them. They were unified.

"How good and pleasant it is when God's people live together in unity" (Ps. 133:1). There's a great difference between unity and uniformity. Watch a company of soldiers on the parade ground and you will see uniformity, but watch them on the battlefield and you will see unity. Unity depends on diversity, and the church must have diversity in order to live and grow. It takes many different gifts and ministries to keep the body functioning. Paul wrote,

> There are different kinds of gifts, but the same Spirit distributes them. There are different kinds of service, but the same Lord. There are different kinds of working, but in all of them and in everyone it is the same God at work. . . . Just as a body, though one, has many parts, but all its many parts form one body, so it is with Christ. (1 Cor. 12:4–6, 12)

Paul used the human body to illustrate unity and diversity. In Psalm 133 the writer used two familiar Jewish similes to illustrate his point: unity is like the anointing oil poured upon the high priest at his consecration (133:2) and like the dew upon the fruitful fields around Mt. Hermon (133:3). The dew was "good" because it watered the crops and helped them to grow, and the oil was "pleasant" because it had a special fragrance that reminded the priest of his special relationship to the Lord.

But that oil flowed *down* Aaron's beard and bathed the breastplate over Aaron's heart, "uniting" the twelve jewels imbedded there. Those jewels represented the twelve tribes of Israel (Exod. 28:15–30). *Uniformity is "worked up" but unity "comes down" from above, like the dew and the oil.* Unity is enjoyed when hearts are yielded to the Holy Spirit, for "the fruit of the Spirit is love" (Gal.5:27).

The phrase "had everything in common" is not a description of "Christian communism" but of Spirit-directed generosity in sacrificial giving. Greedy people say, "What's yours is mine—I'll take it!" But the child of God says, "What's mine is yours—I'll share it." The first extorts by compulsion from the outside; the other gives out of compassion on the inside—the loving power of the Holy Spirit. If we have experienced the grace of God and are walking in the Spirit, we will not have to be pressured to give to the Lord and to those in need. Our giving will be the supernatural result of God's grace at work in our lives. (Read Acts 4:32–35 and 2 Cor. 8–9.)

The Spirit-filled church is not only unified; it is also *magnified.* "They broke bread in their homes and ate bread together with glad and sincere hearts, praising God and enjoying favor with all the people" (Acts 2:47). "No one else dared to join them, even though they were highly regarded by the people" (Acts 5:13). The official religious leaders persecuted the Christians and tried to silence their witness, but the common people watched the believers with amazement and appreciation. In that day the church of Jesus Christ was the only fellowship that welcomed all people regardless of gender, race, social standing, income, reputation, education or achievement. "There is neither

Jew nor Gentile, neither slave nor free, neither male no female, for you are all one in Christ Jesus" (Gal. 3:24). The gracious invitation was and still is, "And everyone who calls on the name of the Lord will be saved" (Acts 2:21).

It's a wonderful thing when the believers in a local church are so radically different from the world that the people in the community have to take notice. "The Church of the Open Door" must never become infected by sin and become "The Church of the Open Sore." In recent years it's been painful to see the reputation of the church greatly stained by the waywardness of a few high-profile Christians. How tragic that many churches have been invaded by division, defilement and outright denial of the faith.

The Spirit allows the church to be magnified when the church magnifies Jesus Christ. "Let your light shine before others, that they may see your good deeds and glorify your Father in heaven" (Matt. 5:16). A church that serves the Lord only during "Sunday services" is failing in its ministry, but when God's people find ways throughout the week to help others in the name of Jesus, that makes a difference. "Religion that God our Father accepts as pure and faultless is this: to look after orphans and widows in their distress and to keep oneself from being polluted by the world" (James 1:27). The early Christians rescued children that were abandoned and exposed to die. They cared for widows and the poor, and sought to love their needy neighbors as Jesus loved them.

When a church is Spirit-filled and Spirit-led, it will not only be unified and magnified, but also *multiplied*. "And the Lord added to their number daily those who were being saved" (Acts 2:47). Jesus said, "I will build my church" (Matt. 16:18), not "I will build *your* church" or "*You* will build my church." It's still true that when God's people do God's work in God's way, God will bless them and be glorified in their ministries. Where there's life, there should be growth: "fruit . . . more fruit . . . much fruit" (John 15:1–5). We desire numbers not because we want to count people but because people count, and we want to reach them and glorify Christ.

---

*There's a difference between bearing fruit and merely achieving results, between building the church and building a crowd.*

---

There's a difference between bearing fruit and merely achieving results, between building the church and building a crowd. Provide attractive religious entertainment and you can build a crowd. Proclaim a popular message that doesn't convict people and you will "get results" and "take in new members." But the Lord wants us to bear fruit, *because fruit involves life and has in it the seeds for more fruit.* If people are truly born again, this new life will be seen in all that they do and will influence others to trust Jesus.

"Not everyone who says to me, 'Lord, Lord,' will enter the kingdom of heaven, but only those who do the will of my Father who is in heaven," said Jesus (Matt. 7:21). It's sad to realize that many who think they are going to heaven will one day be rejected by Jesus (Matt. 7:13, 22). It's also sad to face the fact that sometimes our faulty evangelism helps to create this deception.

During the first great persecution in Jerusalem, the scattered believers "preached the word wherever they went" (Acts 8:4). The word translated "preached" means "to declare the good news, to evangelize." The Christians saw themselves as seeds being dispersed by the tempest, and wherever they landed, they sought to bear fruit. The church of the open door is a growing church because the Holy Spirit is at work in the church family seven days a week. People are praying, sacrificing, serving, sharing the gospel with others, alert to opportunities to magnify Christ.

Os Guinness writes, "Far from leading to an exodus, modern church growth often uses the ideology and tools of Egypt to make the life of the people of God more comfortable in captivity."[5] But when the Holy Spirit really begins to work in and through a church, God's people will face more opportunities than ever before—as well as more opposition.

Let's see what the Enemy does to try to close the doors to our witness.

# 3

## The Church of the Almost Closed Door

THE CHURCH grew daily, with believers meeting in the temple and in private homes, and unbelievers trusting Jesus. The apostles nurtured them in the Scriptures, and the name of Jesus was being magnified. Some of the new Christians from other countries didn't return home at the end of the feast but remained in Jerusalem to be a part of this miracle fellowship. This means they needed places to live and food to eat, both of which were provided by the church family as the people gave sacrificially to the Lord. What glorious days those were!

But whenever God's work is prospering, Satan opposes it. He comes as a lion who devours (1 Pet. 5:8), a serpent who deceives (2 Cor. 11:3) or an accuser who divides (Rev. 12:10–11). You see this vividly recorded in Acts 3–15.

## *The devouring lion (Acts 3–4)*

The traditional hours of prayer at the temple were 9 a.m., 3 p.m., and sunset (see Acts 10:30 and Dan. 6:10), and the Jewish believers honored that tradition. Peter and John probably had often seen this crippled beggar, but that particular day the Spirit told them to do something about the man's plight. At Pentecost God had used Peter and John to win three thousand people to Jesus, yet now they were showing compassion on one man. "The fruit of the Spirit is love" (Gal. 5:22).

The Holy Spirit is mentioned three times in Acts 4 but not once in chapter 3 where the miracle is described; however the Spirit was certainly at work glorifying the name of Jesus. Ten times in these chapters Jesus is mentioned, and His "name" is referred to nine times. The miracle drew a crowd, Peter preached a message, and two thousand more people believed in Jesus Christ and were saved.

---

*The best advertisement for Jesus Christ is the changed lives of those who have trusted Him.*

---

But if the power of the name of Jesus healed this man, *then Jesus must be alive!* That was the kind of proof many of the Jewish religious leaders didn't want, yet they couldn't deny that the beggar had been miraculously healed. The best advertisement for Jesus Christ is the changed lives of those who have trusted Him. Then Satan came as the lion and moved the leaders to arrest and try Peter and John, but the evidence for the defense was too strong, and the leaders had to let them go. They threatened Peter and John and warned them to keep quiet, but the apostles chose to obey God and continue witnessing.

Peter and John returned to "their own people," probably in

the upper room, and reported what had happened, and they all turned to prayer and the Word of God. *Prayer and the Word are spiritual weapons the devil cannot overcome if we use them by faith.* In their praying the believers turned to the Creator (Acts 4:24) and the Law Giver, quoting from Exodus 20:11. They also quoted from Psalm 2:1–2, applying the verses to what both the Romans and the Jews had done in crucifying Jesus (Acts 2:25–28). God had triumphed over His enemies by raising Jesus from the dead, and He would triumph over them again. The believers didn't pray that the persecution would cease so they would have an easier time witnessing. They prayed instead for God's sovereign will to prevail as He gave them power to glorify the name of Jesus. They asked for enablement and not for escape.

The Word of God and prayer go together. Moses delivered God's law to Israel but also met God on Mount Sinai and interceded for his people. The Jewish priests taught the law to the people and also offered the incense in the sanctuary, a symbol of their prayers on their behalf (Deut. 33:10; Ps. 141:2). "As for me," said Samuel, "far be it from me that I should sin against the Lord by failing to pray for you. And I will teach you the way that is good and right" (1 Sam. 12:23).

Prayer and the Word go together. The prophet Daniel learned God's plans from the Scriptures and then prayed that God would fulfill them (Dan. 9:1–3). Our Lord Jesus prayed at the beginning of the day and then went out to teach the Word (Mark 1:35–39). Jesus promised, "If you remain in me and my words remain in you, ask whatever you wish, and it will be done for you" (John 15:7). The apostle Paul wedded the Word and prayer when he blessed the Ephesian elders (Acts 20:32) and in his description of the Christian's spiritual armor (Eph. 6:17–18). What God has joined together we must not separate.

Note in Acts 4:32–35 that the church was still unified, magnified and multiplied.

## *The deceiving serpent (Acts 5)*

Generally speaking, nothing outside the church can defile or defeat the church's walk or witness. It's when the Enemy gets inside the fellowship that he begins to make progress. One disobedient soldier like Achan can bring defeat to the entire army (Josh. 7), and one disobedient believer can defile the whole church (1 Cor. 5). In his second attack on the church, Satan enlisted the help of a husband and wife, Ananias and Sapphira.

Barnabas had given a generous gift to the Lord, so this husband and wife decided to sell a piece of property but give only part of the income to the Lord. Their sin wasn't thievery, because the money was theirs to use as they pleased (Acts 5:4). Their sin was hypocrisy, *trying to make people think they were more spiritual than they really were.* They lied to the Holy Spirit (which proves they were believers) as well as to the people in the church fellowship.

Suppose Peter had not discovered and exposed their deception, and Ananias and Sapphira had remained in the congregation? They would have been admired as generous believers and achieved a reputation for godliness that they didn't deserve. Other believers would have sought their advice and would have received counsel from Satan, not from the Holy Spirit whom they had grieved. Instead of helping to build the church, Ananias and Sapphira would have been secretly destroying it. Spiritual leaders need divine wisdom lest they find themselves cooperating with the devil's plans by endorsing the wrong people.

Note in Acts 5:12–16 that the congregation continued to be unified, magnified and multiplied. The Holy Spirit had won again!

## Again, the devouring lion (Acts 5:17–42)

The continued success of the church ignited the fires of jealousy in the hearts of the official religious leaders, so they arrested all the apostles (5:18, 29, 40) and put them into the public jail. Being Sadducees, the high priest and his friends didn't believe in the resurrection of the human body, including the body of Jesus Christ, and every miracle the apostles performed refuted their false doctrine. Because Jesus was alive and exalted in heaven, His name had power.

They arrested the apostles, but the jail doors didn't remain closed very long, for an angel opened them and commanded the men to return to their ministry in the temple. The high priest summoned the prisoners, but the officers couldn't find them! The apostles were finally discovered in the temple teaching the people, and the guards carefully brought them to the meeting of the Sanhedrin.

What was the charge against the apostles? They had filled Jerusalem with their teaching and were blaming the Sanhedrin for the death of Israel's Messiah (Acts 5:28). The reply of the apostles was to the point: "We must obey God rather than human beings" (Acts 5:29). The council members were furious and wanted to kill the prisoners, but God overruled, and they were flogged, commanded not to preach in the name of Jesus and then released.

The lion had roared but he could neither silence the apostles nor hinder the witness of the church. The apostles rejoiced that they were privileged to suffer for Jesus, and the united church continued to proclaim the gospel in the temple and from house to house, and the number of disciples kept increasing (Acts 6:1).

## The accuser (Acts 6:1–8)

Persecution from the outside the church didn't close the

doors, so Satan attempted once again to create problems inside the church. He had tried deception and failed, and now he would use division, setting the Greek-speaking Jews in the church against the Aramaic-speaking Jews. The widows visiting Jerusalem for the feast and the widows who were native to the land were all being cared for by the church, but some of the women had been neglected. There was now the beginning of conflict in the church, and if people started taking sides, it could lead to a serious division. Jesus said, "Whoever is not with me is against me, and whoever does not gather with me scatters" (Matt. 12:30).

Humanly speaking, who was to blame for this serious problem? The apostles—the leaders—and they admitted it! They were so busy feeding people that they were neglecting the ministry of prayer and the Word of God, and this neglect was depriving the people of the spiritual nourishment and leadership they needed. When the sheep aren't fed spiritually, they start nipping at each other. The solution was simple: with the congregation's approval, the apostles appointed seven men to take care of serving tables, and this released the apostles to focus on the ministry priorities God had given them. There is nothing sinful or humiliating about serving tables, but it could easily be done by people other than the apostles.

---

*Growth in the church is a great blessing, but it can also bring great burdens.*

---

You might call this episode "The Mathematics of Ministry." It begins with *multiplication,* "when the number of disciples was increasing" (Acts 6:1). Growth in the church is a great blessing, but it can also bring great burdens. This multiplication resulted in *division* because there were too many people to care for, so the apostles wisely turned to *subtraction* and willingly relinquished their table responsibilities. This led to *addition,* and seven capable men were assigned to handle the work. The problem was solved! Satan the accuser was defeated! The church was still unified, multiplied and magnified (Acts 6:5–8).

## *The return of the lion (Acts 6:8–9:31)*

Stephen was one of the men appointed to serve tables, but when he wasn't doing that, he was powerfully witnessing in a synagogue frequented by Jewish men from other countries. These men treated Stephen just as Jesus had been treated. They enlisted false witnesses to testify that he had blasphemed against God, Moses and the temple. Stephen's defense was an insightful review of Jewish history, proving that Israel rejected their deliverers the first time and accepted them the second time. This was true of Joseph (7:9–16), Moses (7:17–43) and now Jesus (7:44–53). Unwilling to repent of their sins, the accusers stoned Stephen to death, and he became the first martyr of the Christian church. His life and ministry were closing on earth, but heaven opened to him, and he saw Jesus in His glory.

The death of Stephen was Israel's third murder and a turning point in their history. The leaders sinned against God the Father when they allowed John the Baptist to be slain (Matt. 14:1–12); they sinned against God the Son when they asked for Jesus to be slain (John 19:1–16); and they sinned against God the Holy Spirit (Acts 7:51) when they themselves stoned Stephen. This was their sin against the Spirit of God, and it was final (Matt. 12:30–32). God moved His messengers from Palestine to Samaria and then to the Gentiles, and forty years later, Jerusalem was destroyed.

It was here that Dr. Luke brought Saul/Paul into the story

(Acts 8:1), not only because he was leading the persecution but because the death of Stephen had a profound effect upon him and probably helped to prepare him for conversion (note Acts 22:20). The first twelve chapters of Acts focus primarily on Peter and the rest of the book on the ministry of Paul. Peter had used the "keys of the kingdom" to open the door of faith to the Jews (Acts 2) and to the Samaritans (Acts 8). After he has opened the door of faith for the Gentiles in Acts 10–11 and been delivered from prison in Acts 12, except for an important appearance in Acts 15:7–11, Peter will move off the scene (more about this later).

Once again, Satan the lion failed. The scattering of the saints only enlarged the ministry and prepared the way for the church at Antioch to become the new sending congregation (Acts 11:19–30). God led Barnabas to bring Paul from Tarsus to Antioch, and at Antioch He called them to open the door of faith to the Gentiles in other countries (Acts 14:27). The Lord is sovereign. He moves His servants and "the cloud of blessing" from one place to another and accomplishes His great purposes.

## *The accuser attacks Peter (Acts 10–11)*

Because of their influence on other believers, Satan especially attacks spiritual leaders, and this should encourage us to pray much more for them. Peter would be using the keys for the third and last time as he opened the door of faith to the Gentiles in the land of Palestine (Acts 15:8–11). This would prepare the way for Paul to carry the gospel to Gentiles in other lands.

Because of the wonderful growth of the church in Antioch, which was composed of both Jews and Gentiles (Acts 11:19–30), some of the members of the Jerusalem church believed that those Gentiles had to become Jews before they could become Christians. (Even Peter was still keeping a kosher home: see 10:9–16 and 15:1–2, 24.) This would become the major issue at the Jerusalem conference described in Acts 15, but until now, the churches had not discussed the matter. In a very dramatic way, God taught Peter that the traditional Jewish attitude toward the "unclean Gentiles" was wrong and that he was to take the Gentiles the gospel of God's grace and mix grace and law. God's angel spoke to Cornelius, and God Himself spoke to Peter, so how could Peter resist? His courageous obedience brought salvation to many Gentiles.

But the accuser of the brethren is always on the alert for opportunities to divide the church, and some of the Jewish legalists criticized Peter for what he had done. Peter, however, made it clear that he had done only what God had told him to do, so their problem was with the Lord and not with His servant. God had given Cornelius and his friends and family the same gift of the Spirit He had given to the Jews at Pentecost. *The presence of the Holy Spirit in a person's life is the evidence that the person is born again, and those whom God has accepted must be accepted by other believers.* "Accept one another, then, just as Christ has accepted you, in order to bring praise to God" (Rom. 15:7). Peter's critics did accept the Gentile believers and did praise God (Acts 11:18), and their witness would assist Peter at the critical Jerusalem conference.

## *The lion attacks Peter again (Acts 12)*

Satan the lion is a murderer (John 8:44), and he succeeded in having Herod arrest James, the brother of John, and kill him, making James the first apostle to be martyred. From the human point of view, this was a great loss to the church, but we must remember that Satan cannot take any believer's life without the Lord's permission (Job 2:1–6). James died, not as a victim but as a victor (Rev. 2:10). Missionary leaders tell us that more Christians gave their lives for Christ during the twentieth century than during all the preceding centuries combined. Martyrdom isn't likely to disappear, for as the return of Jesus draws near and Satan's time grows short, our Enemy will intensify his efforts to destroy us (Rev. 12:7–17).

Peter had been imprisoned twice by the Sanhedrin (Acts 4:1–21; 5:17–42), and on the second occasion he and the other apostles were miraculously delivered. Knowing this, Herod assigned sixteen Roman soldiers to guard Peter, four during each of the six-hour shifts. Two would be chained to the prisoner and two would guard the doors (Acts 12:10). This time Peter wasn't going to escape!

But he did escape, and it was the result of the Word of God and prayer. (Remember Acts 6:4?) Peter was sleeping so soundly that the angel had to strike his side to wake him up. (Imagine having an angel for an alarm clock!) If I knew I would be executed the next morning, I wonder how soundly I would sleep the night before. The secret of Peter's peace was the Word Jesus gave him in John 21:18–19, that Peter would grow old and die by crucifixion and not by being beheaded. When Peter was arrested, he rested on that promise—and rested.

But the emphasis in the chapter is on the united praying of the believers in the home of Mary, mother of John Mark. *There is no defeating the power of a praying church!* Take a good look at Dr. Luke's description of this prayer meeting. *Many* believers were there, not just the usual "faithful few." In recent years many churches have cancelled their prayer meetings rather than expanding them and have replaced corporate prayer with "life groups" that focus on matters such as dysfunctional people, crisis recovery and interpersonal relations. These things ought to be addressed biblically, but such groups are not substitutes for the church family meeting regularly for prayer.

Not only were many people present, but they were *united*

in their praying. The burden on their hearts was the deliverance of Peter. They weren't praying generally, "Lord, bless Peter!" but very specifically, "Lord, deliver Peter!" Even more, they prayed *earnestly*. The word translated "earnestly" in verse 5 is used to describe our Lord's praying in Luke 22:44, when His "sweat was like drops of blood falling to the ground." We need to be like the Colossian church leader Epaphras who was "always wrestling in prayer" for the people of God (Col. 4:12). The word translated "wrestling" gives us our English word "agonize." It described a determined runner striving to reach the finish line.

It was *persistent* prayer, throughout the week and all through the night. They didn't ask somebody to "lead in prayer" and then go home when the prayer was ended. They remained together that night, interceding for Peter. When our hearts are truly burdened, we pay little attention to time. I recall what a blessing our Youth for Christ all-night prayer meetings were at our annual conventions and how the Lord heard and answered, to His glory. I also recall as a young Christian attending pre service prayer meetings at church each Sunday morning and evening. When I began to preach, what an encouragement it was before the service when God's people laid their hands on me and prayed. Do churches still do that, or are we too busy setting the levels on the sound system?

God answered their prayers and delivered Peter. The prison doors opened for him, *but he couldn't get through the door and into the prayer meeting at Mary's house!* Their praying was sincere, but when God sent the answer, their faith was small, and Peter was kept outside! They remind us of the words of the distraught father who brought his demonized son to Jesus: "I do believe; help me overcome my unbelief" (Mark 9:24). God also took the life of arrogant King Herod and blessed the church's ministry of the Word. (Acts 12:18–24).

In spite of the group's weak faith, they overcame Satan by the Word of God and prayer. This entire episode reminds me of Psalm 34:15–16, which Peter quoted in First Peter 3:12—"For the eyes of the Lord are on the righteous and his ears are attentive to their prayer, but the face of the Lord is against those who do evil." Satan the lion did not conquer, but the Lion of Judah did, and He still conquers when His people take "the sword of the Spirit, which is the word of God" and "pray in the Spirit" (Eph. 6:17–18). However, the Enemy didn't give up but returned to attack again as the serpent. This why believers must "pray continually" (1 Thess. 5:17) and use the sword of the Spirit constantly, for those are the weapons that defeat Satan and keep the doors of ministry open.

## Satan the serpent and the lion (Acts 13–15)

This section covers Paul's first missionary journey and the conference at Jerusalem. Note that "Barnabas and Saul" (13:2) received their call while engaged in worship and fasting and that they were sent out by the Holy Spirit through the local church (13:2–4). What began as "Barnabas and Saul" eventually became "Paul and his companions" (13:13) and ultimately "Paul and Barnabas" (13:42; 14:1; but see 15:25).

It isn't unusual in Christian work that the founders of ministries don't always remain as the leaders. Some servants are excellent obstetricians and can "give birth" to ministries, but then a "pediatrician" is needed to help it continue and grow. Both are important, and wise are the leaders who know their own gifts and calling. That Paul changed his name from Saul to Paul is significant (Acts 13:9), for the Latin word *paulus* means "little, small." He had the humble attitude of John the Baptist who said, "He [Jesus] must become greater; I must become less" (John 3:30).

All of us need that attitude. Everything in church ministry rises and falls with godly leadership, and the Lord has the privilege of appointing leaders as He desires. It's often very difficult for founding leaders to step aside and allow another to take over, but these changes have to take place. As with Moses and Joshua, some leaders know who their successors are and prepare them, but that isn't always the case. Sometimes an obvious leader arises and is immediately recognized, but often there must be a search involving much patience and prayer.

---

*Wherever God plants true servants of the kingdom to bear fruit, Satan plants counterfeits, "children of the devil."*

---

We learn from Christ's "Parable of the Tares" (Matt. 13:24–30, 36–43) that wherever God plants true servants of the kingdom to bear fruit, Satan plants counterfeits, "children of the devil." Both John the Baptist and Jesus confronted the scribes and Pharisees and identified them as Satan's servants (Matt. 3:7–10; John 8:44), and on Cyprus Paul confronted Elymas the sorcerer and identified him as "a child of the devil" (Acts 13:10). *Satan the serpent was at work.*

But as Paul and his companions continued their travels, it was Satan the lion who followed them. At Antioch in Pisidia, Paul had great success, but the Jews openly opposed him (Acts 13:44–45, 49–51), and at Iconium the unbelievers plotted to stone them, so Paul and his friends left. At first the people at Lystra treated Paul and Barnabas like gods, but when unbelievers from Antioch and Iconium arrived, the same crowd stoned Paul and left him for dead. The Lord raised him up, he went back into the city, and he and his companions revisited the new churches as they made their way back to their "sending church" in Antioch of Syria. "On arriving there, they gathered the church together and reported all that God had done through them and how he had opened a door of faith to the Gentiles" (Acts 14:27). It was still the church of the open door, and the word spread that Gentiles throughout the Roman Empire were being saved.

But Satan the serpent was ready to strike again. We've noted that when Satan the lion attacks from outside the church, he rarely succeeds, because persecution usually purifies the church and energizes it for witnessing. Therefore, Satan follows persecution with an attack *inside the church* and often succeeds in causing confusion and division. In the Jerusalem church certain Pharisees who had believed in Jesus were teaching that the Gentiles had to become Jews before they could become genuine Christians (Acts 15:1–5). This meant accepting Judaism and its laws and proving it by being circumcised. If they were correct, then the Gentiles that Paul and Barnabas and the scattered believers had led to faith in Christ were not truly born again, and their baptism was fraudulent. In short, they were not Christians!

Because the church at Antioch had a large Gentile constituency, some of these legalists went there and began to spread their teachings. Paul and Barnabas disputed with them, but the visitors wouldn't give in, so it was decided that Paul and Barnabas go to Jerusalem with them, and with some members of the church in Antioch, and discuss the matter with the apostles and elders. This was not a "church council" in the historic sense because not all the churches were involved. It was more like a "committee of the whole" as the key leaders assembled to examine a specific problem and make a decision that would be binding on all the churches.

After a great deal of discussion (and dispute) among the leaders, Peter reminded them of what the Lord had done in the past when he preached to Cornelius and his family and friends

(Acts 13:6–11; 10:1–11:18). In the home of Cornelius, God gave the Gentiles the same Holy Spirit He had given the Jewish believers at Pentecost, so these people must have been truly born again, totally apart from Judaism. Then Paul and Barnabas spoke about the present works of God, about how He had saved the Gentiles in city after city through their ministry, attesting to its authenticity by giving signs and wonders (Acts 15:12). James summarized what had been said and then gave his conclusion. He was the half-brother of Jesus and the leader of the Jerusalem congregation.

James started with doctrine and affirmed that the salvation of the Gentiles apart from the law of Moses was not contrary to anything written in the law or the prophets, and he quoted Amos 9:11–12 to prove it. As Peter had said, Jews were saved by faith, apart from the law, just like Gentiles (Acts 15:11). Then James moved from doctrine to duty. He said that, though the Gentiles didn't need to obey the law to be saved, they shouldn't deliberately dishonor or demean the law, lest they offend the believing Jews or hinder the unbelieving Jews from turning to Christ. A good Christian should be a good example.

James specifically mentioned that the saved Gentiles should obey God's commands by avoiding immorality and idolatry. They should also make two concessions to the Jews by not eating meat from strangled animals or blood from any animal. These concessions had nothing to do with salvation, but they would help to remove obstacles that might keep unsaved Jews from trusting Christ.

There's another aspect of this matter that must not be ignored. By insisting that the Gentiles obey the law of Moses, the legalists were trying to transplant Jewish culture where the Lord had never commanded it to go. Much that is found in the Jewish law is cultural, not theological, and was never given to the

Gentiles to obey. "He has revealed his word to Jacob, his laws and decrees to Israel. He has done this for no other nation; they do not know his laws" (Psalm 147:19–20).

World evangelism doesn't mean exporting American culture, British culture or any other national culture. Evangelism means telling people about Jesus and His gracious salvation. Once people are saved, they will work out their own salvation as the Spirit directs them (Phil. 2:12–13) and express their faith in a manner suited to their own cultural heritage.

The apostle Paul was not only the servant of Jesus Christ and His church (Col. 1:7, 25), but he was also the servant of the gospel itself (Col. 1:23). *His life and ministry didn't contradict the message that he proclaimed, nor should ours.* The gospel is a message for the whole world; therefore, it cannot become the exclusive property of one people or group. The gospel is a simple message and a free message and must not become entangled with regulations and rituals that overshadow the grace of God.

---

*The gospel is a message of sacrifice and love, and we who preach it must be willing to pay a price to reach others.*

---

The gospel is a message of sacrifice and love, and we who preach it must be willing to pay a price to reach others (Acts 15:25–26). When you don't proclaim the gospel of Jesus Christ, you can do anything you please in your life and "ministry" because your message is false. But if you preach the true gospel, you must live a true life.

Paul, Barnabas, Judas and Silas carried the "decrees" of the conference to the Gentiles in the churches in Antioch, Syria and Cilicia, and once again the believers rejoiced in God's grace and were unified and multiplied. But Satan didn't call off his attack, for if he couldn't close the door of faith to the Gentiles, he would keep the ambassadors from going through the door. The Scottish preacher Andrew Bonar said, "We must be as watchful after the victory as before the battle," and this is good counsel for all believers, not just missionaries.

## Satan the accuser (Acts 15:36–41)

When it came to matters theological, Paul and Barnabas agreed; but when it came to matters personal and practical, they disagreed. They had "a sharp disagreement" (the same word as in Acts 15:2) over John Mark, who had deserted them during their first missionary journey (Acts 13:13). Paul and Barnabas couldn't resolve their differences, so they parted company. Paul chose Silas to be his new partner and with him retraced the route of his first missionary journey, while Barnabas and Mark sailed to Cyprus to serve. Now there were two "teams" ministering instead of one.

We don't have a transcript of the heated discussion, but it's clear that Paul and Barnabas were looking at Mark from two different perspectives. Paul was asking, "What can Mark do for the work?" and Barnabas was asking, "What can the work do for Mark?" Both questions are important and both are not always easy to answer, but in choosing personnel both must be considered. Neither John Mark nor Barnabas is mentioned again in the Book of Acts, but if we correctly understand Colossians 4:10, Philemon 24 and Second Timothy 4:11, Paul later forgave Mark and admitted that he was a profitable servant of God. Grace triumphed over law, and the accuser was silenced.

In local church ministry there are people like John Mark who end well even though they didn't begin well, and we need to be patient and prayerful as we help them. There are also people who begin well and don't end well; they go up like a rocket and come down like a rock. Dr. Martyn Lloyd-Jones once said to me, "It's tragic when people succeed before they are ready for it." We should seek to reclaim them, if possible, and watch ourselves lest we follow their bad example.

Personal differences in local churches and other ministries shouldn't discourage us, because they occur in every organization— the armed forces, government, colleges and universities, and even the best of families. Satan is busy scattering while Jesus is gathering (Luke 11:23). Our Lord is bringing things together (Eph. 1:10) while Satan is tearing things apart. If we belong to Jesus, our task is to "make every effort to keep the unity of the Spirit through the bond of peace" (Eph. 4:3). The spiritual unity is already there; our privilege and obligation is to protect and maintain it in love. We aren't always right, nor are we always wrong; but we can be "always . . . praying for all the saints" (Eph. 6:18), and we can always give ourselves fully to the work of the Lord, because we know that our labor in the Lord is not in vain (1 Cor. 15:58).

## Open and closed doors (Acts 16–28)

A survey of these thirteen chapters reveals that God's people repeatedly faced open doors of opportunity and that each opportunity invited Satan to put obstacles in the way to discourage them and make them want to quit. If we walk by sight, we will be overcome; if we walk by faith, we will be overcomers. (Later we will look at Revelation 2–3 and discover what it means to be an overcomer.) Paul had the right idea: "But I will stay on at Ephesus until Pentecost, because a great door for effective work has opened to me, and there are many who oppose me" (1 Cor. 16:8–9). Here's the sequence: open doors—opportunities—obstacles—overcomers.

As Paul started his second missionary journey, it looked like the doors were shut, but then the door opened to Macedonia. Speaking to a small group of women at a riverside prayer meeting didn't seem exciting, but it led to the founding of the church in Philippi, which I believe was Paul's favorite church. God opened Lydia's heart, Lydia opened her home, and then the Enemy put Paul and Silas behind locked doors in prison. But their prayers and hymns reached God's throne, and He sent an earthquake. (Remember the shaking of the house in Acts 4:31?) The prisoners' chains came loose, the prison doors flew open, and Paul led the jailer and his family to faith in Christ, and perhaps some of the prisoners as well.

Paul and Silas refused to sneak out of town like guilty criminals but insisted that the Roman officials come personally, escort them out of jail and apologize for what they had done. Had Paul not taken this approach, the infant church in Philippi would always have been under a perpetual cloud of suspicion. The Roman officers knew that Paul was right and willingly cooperated. As Paul and his companions traveled on, each new city presented a different challenge, and they had to exercise Spirit-given discernment.

The team was in Thessalonica less than a month when a mob attacked the house of Jason their host, so Paul and Silas were whisked away to Berea. There the people were much more open to the Word, but then the troublemakers from Thessalonica arrived and stirred up the people, so Paul left for Athens by himself. He did have some fruit in Athens but then left for Corinth where Silas and Timothy joined him. They remained there probably eighteen months, and a church was established. Paul's first letter to the Corinthians reveals that the church had more than its share of problems, but Paul patiently tried to help solve them. Paul left Corinth for Ephesus where he had a remarkable ministry for about three years. It ended with a citywide riot, but during those years "all the Jews and Greeks who lived in Asia heard the word of the Lord" (Acts 19:10).

Paul's next destination was Jerusalem where he was falsely accused of bringing Gentiles into the temple, and an uprising occurred. Paul was dragged out of the temple and the gates were shut (Acts 21:30). Closed doors! Those gates were never opened to him again because he was arrested and kept under guard for two years in Caesarea. After trials before the Jewish Sanhedrin, Felix the governor, Festus his successor and King Agrippa, Paul was sent to Rome to be tried before Caesar. He went through a storm and shipwreck before arriving in Rome and lived in his own rented house for two years as he awaited trial (Acts 28:11–31). Paul was under guard *but the doors were still open, and he shared the Word of God with all who came "with all boldness and without hindrance"!*

---

*The Book of Acts opens with the church behind closed doors.*

---

The Book of Acts opens with the church behind closed doors, but it ends with open doors in Rome and Paul willing to speak to any and all who visit him. Between chapter 1 and chapter 28, doors open and close and open again, and the believers take advantage of the opportunities God gives them. No matter how discouraging the problems or distressing the circumstances, our faith in the Lord and our courage and obedience can turn obstacles into opportunities, and we can be overcomers to the glory of Jesus Christ.

# 4

~~∞~~

# The Ephesian Emphasis,
# Part 1

IF WE WERE playing a word-association game and the leader announced the word "Paul," you would hear different responses from the players, such as "apostle," "missionary," "theologian" or perhaps "writer," all of which would be acceptable. But it's unlikely that any player would reply "pastor," because we don't usually think of Paul as the pastor of a local congregation. The average Christian envisions Paul as a busy missionary who suddenly arrives in a city, preaches the gospel, sometimes creates a riot, and after a few days or weeks leaves town, sometimes when nobody is watching. Between his arrival and departure, he might even spend a few nights in jail.

But that description is really a caricature, because Paul was indeed a pastor who organized local churches and either in person, by epistle or through one of his associates, lovingly shepherded the people he had won to Christ. In Second Corinthans

11:28 he wrote, "I face daily the pressure of my concern for all the churches." He spent eighteen months in Corinth and almost three years in Ephesus; but even if he remained only a few weeks in a city, before he left he had formed a body of saved people to serve Jesus in that place.

Paul's ministry at Ephesus interests me for at least four reasons. First, it was Paul's longest pastorate, at least three years. Second, during his ministry there, the church at Ephesus reached "all Asia" with the gospel (Acts 19:10, 26). Of course, that means the Roman province of Asia and not what we know today as the continent of Asia. Third, the Lord gave "extraordinary miracles" to attest the ministry (20:11–12). My fourth reason is most important: the Lord gave four special communications to the Ephesian congregation and leaders, communications that are very important to us today. They are: Paul's farewell speech to the elders (Acts 20:17–38); the two epistles to Timothy, who was Paul's apostolic representative in Ephesus; and the Spirit's letter to the Ephesian church in Revelation 2:1–7. These messages are important to us today if we want to serve through incarnation and not imitation and so build biblical ministries that God can bless.

## *The Farewell Address (Acts 20:17–38)*

Paul was on his way to Jerusalem to deliver the offering he had collected from the Gentile churches for the poor Jewish believers. Rather than take time to detour to Ephesus, Paul invited the elders of the Ephesian church to meet him at Miletus where he delivered a "farewell message" that teaches us a great deal about faithful Christian ministry. Giving is one of the key themes of his message. In fact, Paul's "text" could have been the words of Jesus quoted in verse 35, "It is more blessed to give than to receive." Using this as our theme, we may outline the message this way:

The past: Paul gave his best at Ephesus (20:17–21)

The future: Paul will give his life if necessary (20:22–27)

The present: Paul gives directions to the elders (20:28–31)

The benediction: Paul gives his blessing to all (20:32–35)

Ministering means serving, serving means giving, and giving means sacrificing. Both Jesus Christ and Paul are examples of the sacrificial ministry described in this message. "Keep watch over yourselves and all the flock of which the Holy Spirit has made you overseers," Paul admonished. "Be shepherds of the church of God which he bought with his own blood" (20:28). The hireling asks, "How much will I get?" while the true shepherd says, "I will give all that I have" (John 10:11–13). True shepherds don't count the cost. To them it is worth searching for and finding even one lost sheep and bringing it back to the fold.

---

*Ministering means serving, serving means giving,*
*and giving means sacrificing.*

---

Note the key image Paul used: the church is God's flock and the elders are shepherds (20:28–29). It's been suggested by some that the word "shepherd" (pastor) be eliminated from our vocabulary because it smacks of rural scenery rather than our current urban culture. Yet Paul used the words *shepherd* and *flock* to instruct and encourage church leaders working in *a city of 300,000 citizens!* Ephesus was an urban center that ranked third in the empire for political power, yet *Paul used these "rural" images without apology.* He didn't think the shepherd metaphor was irrelevant and belonged only to a rural milieu.

*Instead of eliminating the shepherd image, it needs to be emphasized today as never before.* Even in our great cities sinners are still lost sheep that must be found; and in our churches saints are still lambs and sheep who need to be fed, led and protected. The church is not a business "run" by CEOs and "leadership teams." It's still a flock of sheep and must be led, not driven.

Should we remove the shepherd image from Scripture? If we do, we eliminate Abel, Abraham, Isaac, Jacob and Joseph (there goes the Pentateuch!), David and a host of psalms, including the Twenty-third. We will lose Isaiah 53 and numerous other passages in the Prophets, and also many New Testament passages, such as the Parable of the Lost Sheep, and Jesus the Good Shepherd (John 10), the Great Shepherd (Heb. 13:20–21) and the Chief Shepherd (1 Peter 5:1–4). Jesus will one day "shepherd" the nations as well as shepherd His people in heaven (Rev. 2:27; 7:17; 12:5; 19:15). What happens to the doctrine of the atonement if the Shepherd doesn't lay down His life for the sheep? And what happens to pastoral care? Peter wrote, "Be shepherds of God's flock that is under your care, watching over them . . . being examples to the flock" (1 Pet. 5:2–3). Are we to remove that admonition from our Bibles?

Now let's look at Paul's message.

## The past: Paul gave his best at Ephesus (20:17–21)

He gave his best because he humbly served the Lord (20:19). The word translated "served" means "to serve as a bondslave" and not as a superior executive. The Old Testament priests served the people, but they first served the Lord (Exod. 28:1–4; 19:1), and we serve the people of God because we serve the God who loves those people. He loves them through us. Paul lived a consistent life (20:18) and a humble and courageous life (20:19). *Paul worked hard as he ministered, and so should we.* Whether in public preaching to crowds or in ministry to "house churches," families and individuals in homes, Paul was busy sharing the Word of God. Paul had time for individuals. That's a mark of a faithful shepherd.

Paul knew what it meant to have a broken heart. Real men aren't supposed to weep, but Paul wept and wasn't ashamed of it (20:19, 31, 37). He not only wept over the church but also over the lost (Rom. 9:2) and over worldly professed Christians in the church (Phil. 3:18). Even though his life was often in danger, he didn't weep for himself but only for those he was seeking to win and to edify. We don't hear much weeping in churches today, although there's often a good deal of laughter.

The word "fun" has moved into the church's vocabulary of late, probably because hymns that encourage reverence and "the fear of the Lord" have moved out. I walked into a church one Sunday morning, and a "greeter" shook my hand and said, "Welcome! Come in and have fun!"

As kindly as I could, I told him I attended church to worship the Lord and not to have fun, and then I asked him to show me the word "fun" in the Bible. Open-mouthed, he stared at me and said nothing. To him the sanctuary was a theater, and worship was supposed to be entertainment. He needed to ponder James 4:9—"Grieve, mourn and wail. Change your laughter into mourning and your joy to gloom." If you're in ministry, you need a healthy sense of humor and the joy of the Lord, but your calling isn't to entertain the goats or make the sheep laugh.

Paul had a balanced ministry (20:20–21). He preached the Word to Jews and to Gentiles, and he called for repentance and faith. This means he confronted his listeners with the fact of sin and the good news of salvation through faith in Jesus Christ. Repentance without faith is misery, and faith without repentance is vanity. Paul wasn't a crowd pleaser who avoided the bad news of sin and judgment that must always prepare the way for the good news of faith and forgiveness.

The verb "hesitated" (20:20) describes an army in fear retreating from the battle. But Paul marched right on and spoke the truth, no matter who might be offended. The word "preach" (20:20) describes a messenger giving an official announcement that must be heard and obeyed. The preacher is the messenger of the King of Kings, and he doesn't manufacture his message—he declares it.

---

*Paul wasn't afraid of the future, for the future is your friend when Jesus is your Lord.*

---

## *The future: Paul will give his life if necessary (20:22–27)*

Dr. Luke wrote two books about "going to Jerusalem." In the Gospel of Luke, he described our Lord's journey to Jerusalem (Luke 9:31, 51–53), and in the Acts of the Apostles, he described Paul's journey to Jerusalem, which eventually led to his journey to Rome. (Paul wasn't afraid of the future, for the future is your friend when Jesus is your Lord.) In this brief testimony Paul gives us six pictures of his life as a faithful Christian servant.

To begin with, God's servants are *accountants* (20:24). "I consider my life worth nothing to me" reminds us of what Paul wrote to the Philippian believers in Philippians 3:7–9. Paul is dealing with values, as every dedicated believer must do. Because Moses had the right values, he turned his back on Egypt, identified with God's suffering people and rescued the nation of Israel (Heb. 11:24–26). This was a lesson Peter had to learn (Matt. 16:21–26), and so must we.

We are also *runners in the race* (20:24). Paul wanted to end well, and he did (2 Tim. 4:7–8). In the ancient Greek Olympics, there were only first-place winners; there were no awards for second or third. Believers are not competing against each other; we are competing with ourselves and seeking to do better as we run the race (Phil. 3:12–14; Heb. 12:1–3). God equips us for the race and enables us to reach the goal if we run by faith and obey the rules (2 Tim. 2:5). Each of us must have the discipline and determination of the finest athlete, or we will end up disqualified (1 Cor. 9:24–27).

Paul also saw himself as a *steward* (20:24). He wanted to "complete the task" that the Lord Jesus had given him. "A person can receive only what is given from heaven," said John the Baptist when people tried to make him and Jesus look like competitors (John 3:26–30). Each of us has been given spiritual gifts, natural abilities and definite opportunities for serving Christ. This is our stewardship, and "it is required that those who have been given a trust must prove faithful" (1 Cor. 4:2).

Successful stewards are faithful stewards. They don't waste their lives or spend their lives, but invest their lives in that which matters most—pleasing their Master. It's a privilege to be the Lord's steward, but it's also a great responsibility, because one day we must stand at the judgment seat of Christ to give account of our service (Rom. 14:10–12; 2 Cor. 5:10).

As a preacher, Paul realized that he was a *witness* and a *herald* (20:24–25). The word translated "testify" means "to solemnly witness," while the word translated "preaching" describes the herald of the king delivering his message. Witnesses are people who tell what they have seen and heard, while royal heralds declare what the king has told them to declare. The judge and jury aren't the least interested in what the witnesses think about the case, because they want to hear only the facts; and the citizens want to hear what the king has told the herald to tell them. The herald represents the ruler and must declare everything commanded by his master. "For I have not hesitated to proclaim to you the whole will of God" (20:27). The preacher who trims the message just to please the crowd will displease his Master and rob his hearers of the truths they desperately need to hear.

Finally, Paul realized he was *a watchman* (20:26). This is an image taken from Ezekiel 3:17–21 and 33:1–9, where the Lord made the prophet a watchman on the walls and commanded him to keep his eyes open and warn the people when danger was approaching. If the watchman failed to do his job and the city was taken, the blood of those slain was on his hands. During his ministry in Ephesus, Paul was a faithful watchman who was therefore "innocent of the blood of everyone" (20:26).

"So be on your guard!" he warned the elders. "Remember that for three years I never stopped warning each of you night and day with tears" (20:31). The prophet Isaiah pictured unfaithful watchmen as blind dogs who were asleep and couldn't bark (Isa. 56:10–13)! Of what good are they?

Paul knew that trials awaited him and perhaps even martyrdom, but he faced the future with confidence because he had been faithful in his ministry. The faithful servant need never fear giving account at the judgment seat of Christ where the rewards will be distributed. The question isn't are we successful? Only God can accurately measure success. The question is are we faithful? Faithfulness is the one quality God looks for in a steward (1 Cor. 4:2, 5).

## The present: Paul gives directions to the elders (20:28–31)

Never underestimate the importance of the local church. According to 20:28, it is the "church of God" (the Father), purchased by the blood of God the Son and superintended by God the Holy Spirit. The entire Godhead is involved! Local churches are so important that Satan attacks them from within and from without (the serpent and the lion) in his attempts to destroy God's work. This is why Paul admonished spiritual leaders to

"Keep watch over yourselves and all the flock" (20:28), which simply means, "Be faithful shepherds" (see 1 Tim. 4:15–16). If the spiritual leaders of the church don't cultivate a disciplined and devoted walk with the Lord, how can they lead the church in the will of God? One of the most important keys to success in any godly endeavor is faithful spiritual leadership.

I thank God for the effective work being done by various Christian ministries in today's challenging world, but at the foundation of God's work is "the church of the living God, the pillar and the foundation of the truth" (1 Tim. 3:15). It's been my privilege to pastor three churches and to minister in and with many evangelical organizations—mission boards, publishers, seminaries, radio ministries, outreaches to children, teenagers and college students, to name a few—and I have never forgotten that these ministries are part of the church and not substitutes for the church.

---

*We must use our gifts where God puts us, but no individual worker can do everything; so we labor together to accomplish the will of God.*

---

I don't like the word "parachurch" because it suggests that the people in these organizations are "alongside the church" but not in it, and that's not true. All true believers belong to the Body of Christ, and no matter what our *base* of ministry is, we should work together for the truth in our various *spheres* of ministry (3 John 8). We must use our gifts where God puts us, but no individual worker can do everything; so we labor together to accomplish the will of God (John 4:34–38). The world calls it "networking"; Paul called it being "laborers together with God" (1 Cor. 3:6–9).

Note the three titles used for these local church leaders: elders (presbyters, 20:17), which suggests spiritual maturity and experience; bishops or overseers (20:28), which defines their major ministry, watching over the people and work of the Lord; and pastors (shepherds, 20:28), which speaks of leading, feeding and protecting. One godly and very effective pastor told me, "If we took our eyes off this ministry for one day, the devil would find a way to start destroying it." No wonder Paul said, "Be on your guard!" (20:31).

Paul warned them of dangers from outside the church, the "wolves" that wanted to come in and destroy the sheep (20:29). Jesus had given a similar warning to His disciples (Matt. 7:15; 10:16; Luke 10:3). When the wolves in sheep's clothing show up, the hirelings flee (John 10:12), but the shepherds remain on duty and protect the flock at any cost. There are all sorts of counterfeit Christians who want to invade the church and exploit it (2 Cor. 11:13–15; 2 Pet. 2:1–3), and the elders must be on guard. Peter said that these "wolves" would "secretly introduce destructive heresies" (2 Pet. 3:1–3), and Jude warned that they would "secretly slip in" and pervert the grace of God by permitting immorality (Jude 3–4). How many warnings do we need?

But there are also dangers *among* us, "even from your own number" (20:30). Some of these enemies undermine the doctrinal foundation of the ministry. John called these people "antichrists" (1 John 2:18–19; 4:1–6), people already in the church fellowship who don't believe the truth and eventually have to leave. The church must never compromise its doctrinal position just to please people and increase membership. We are urged to "contend for the faith that the Lord has once for all entrusted to us, his people" (Jude 3). When leaders start tinkering with the doctrinal statement, it may mean they have a hidden agenda.

One of the most dangerous persons in the church is the one who "loves to be first" (3 John 9) and wants to be in charge of everything. Diotrephes had rejected John's apostolic authority, the authority of the associates John had sent to the church, and also the members of the church who received John's messengers. Today we would call this "secondary separation," and it is unbiblical. As evil as doctrinal heresy is, I believe that more damage has been done by "church bosses" and "first families" than perhaps by any other strategy of the devil. Humility is required of leaders, and their example is the Lord Jesus Christ (Phil. 2:1–12).

Night and day Paul had warned them about these dangers, and we need to heed his warnings today.

---

*Unless leaders spend time daily in the Word and prayer and allow that Word to nourish and guide them and their people, the church will be managed in a worldly manner.*

---

## The benediction: Paul gives his blessing to all (20:32–38)

In these final words Paul sounds a good deal like the prophet Samuel when he said farewell to the people of Israel, who had decided to replace him with a king (1 Sam. 12). Paul commended them to God (prayer) and to God's Word—the Word of God and prayer (see 1 Sam. 12:23 and Acts 6:4)—for he knew that the elders could never minister effectively in their own strength and wisdom. The fact that believers are bank presidents or have degrees in management doesn't necessarily mean they are spiritually qualified to "take care of God's church" (1 Tim. 3:5). Unless leaders spend time daily in the Word and prayer and allow that Word to nourish and guide them and their people, the church will be managed in a worldly manner. It may seem very successful to the people and yet be a great failure in the sight of God.

In his closing words Paul pointed out several "leadership sins" that must be avoided by those who are serving as shepherds of the flock. The first is *covetousness* (20:33), that hidden appetite for praise, wealth, authority and a host of other things that take the place of the glory of God and the will of God. Even an unhealthy craving for a "big church" can destroy the work of God, because covetousness is idolatry (Eph. 5:5), and God will not step aside for idols, especially the "golden idol" of money.

God's laborers are worthy of support (Luke 10:7; Gal. 6:6; 2 Tim. 2:6), especially those who teach the Word and administer the affairs of the church (1 Tim. 5:17), but Paul chose to set aside these rights so that nobody could accuse him of using the ministry as a means to get money out of people (1 Cor. 9; 1 Thess. 2:1–12). He didn't say that all ministers should pay their own way as he did, but it's a good attitude to have, even if we do accept a paycheck we've rightfully earned. Paul accepted gifts from churches and individuals, but he usually shared them with his associates in ministry. The point I'm making is that servants of God must be very careful not to dirty their hands with "dishonest gain" ("filthy lucre," Titus 1:7, 11 and 1 Pet. 5:2, KJV).

I have already mentioned that this address presents Paul as a hard worker who served day and night and knew something about tears and trials. "In everything I did, I showed you that by this kind of hard work we must help the weak" (20:35). He wrote to the churches in Rome, "Never be lacking in zeal, but keep your spiritual fervor, serving the Lord" (Rom. 12:11).

If the closing scene (20:36–38) doesn't touch our hearts, something is radically wrong with us. Paul prayed for his dear friends, in love they embraced one another and wept, they walked to the ship, and Paul and his companions had to "tear themselves away" (21:1). The tie is strong and sensitive that binds shepherds and their sheep, and that's what makes it so difficult to say goodbye.

# 5

The Ephesian Emphasis,
Part 2

PAUL WAS a prisoner in Rome when he wrote Ephesians
(3:1; 4:1; 6:20). Most students believe it was a circular letter
sent to the churches that were founded during Paul's three-year
ministry in Ephesus (Acts 19:10). It may not read like a pastor's
manual, but an understanding of Ephesians is essential for an
effective ministry in the local church.

We can't do without the Pastoral Epistles, of course, but
Ephesians helps us grasp the big picture of what God is doing
in this world. The very format of the letter is an example of balanced ministry: the first three chapters focus on doctrine and the
last three on duty. It's important to understand what God has
done for us, but it's also important to know what He wants us to
do for Him. There are many professed believers today who can
explain doctrine but don't pay much attention to duty.

Some years ago I happened to meet a Christian musician friend of mine in Chicago's O'Hare Field, and I asked him where he had been ministering. He named a popular Christian conference center and mentioned the name of the speaker for that week, a man I knew.

"What did he preach about?" I asked, and my friend replied, "He taught Ephesians. He was in the heavenlies all week and never did come down to earth where we live."

Like too many preachers, the speaker was so wrapped up in the doctrinal that he forgot the practical. He should have included both in his messages.

---

*One of the aims of the Ephesian letter is to explain how God, through the church, will "bring unity to all things in heaven and on earth under Christ."*

---

One of the aims of the Ephesian letter is to explain how God, through the church, will "bring unity to all things in heaven and on earth under Christ" (1:10). The church has been given the message and ministry of reconciliation for a society that is shattered by sin (2 Cor. 5:11–6:2). In Ephesians Paul applies the truth of reconciliation in three areas: sinners being reconciled to God (1:1–2:10), Jews and Gentiles being reconciled to each other in Christ (2:10–3:13) and Christians being reconciled to one another in the church (4:1–5:21), in the home (5:22–6:4) and in the workplace (6:5–9). The only place where there is no reconciliation is on the battlefield where we stand up against Satan and his hosts (6:10–20).

Through His obedient people Jesus is "gathering" things together, but Satan is dividing and scattering (Matt. 12:30). If all true believers in local churches were obeying what Christ has commanded, there would be more unity in this world and less division, more light and less darkness, and more salt and less decay. The problem isn't that sinners are acting like sinners—you expect that—but that saints are acting like sinners! Before God judges the sinners in this world, He will judge sinners in the church, "For it is time for judgment to begin with God's household" (1 Pet. 4:17; see also Prov. 11:31 and Ezek. 9:1–6). After all, "from the one who has been entrusted with much, much more will be asked" (Luke 12:48).

There are several approaches we can take to this marvelous letter, but I want to focus on the images of the church that Paul uses and the practical ministerial truths they teach us. As Christians, we are appealing to broken people in a broken world to be reconciled to God (2 Cor. 5:18–20), and to believers in divided churches and families to love one another.

## *The family (Eph. 1:5)*

This image is found in the word *adoption,* which means "placed as an adult member of the family." We don't enter God's family through adoption but through regeneration, being *born again* by the Spirit of God (John 3:1–15; 1 Pet. 1:22–25). Adopted children can receive the family name, live in the family home and even inherit the family wealth, *but they don't possess the family nature.* That comes only through birth, and we receive God's nature only by faith in Jesus Christ (2 Pet. 1:1–4). When we trust the Savior, we become children of God and are expected to progress from "little children" to mature people of God (2 Pet. 3:18; 1 John 2:12–14).

But *adoption* teaches us that the instant we trusted Jesus as our Savior, the Father gave each of us an adult standing in His wonderful family. Why? Because He wants all His divine resources to be available to us so we can draw upon them and start maturing and becoming more like Christ. Babies are severely limited when it comes to the necessary functions of life, and as they get older, they master these functions. But the Father gives His spiritual children "everything we need for a godly life" (2 Pet. 1:3) when He gives us an adult standing in the family.

For example, babies are able to cry but they aren't able to speak any language; yet when we were born again, the Spirit brought about our adoption and we said, "Abba, Father" (Rom. 8:14–16). Babies don't know they are babies, or even that they are human, and at birth they certainly don't know the meaning of the words "father" or "mother," but believers *know* they are God's children and that God is their Father (Gal. 4:6; 1 John 5:13).

Paul in Ephesians has much to say about speech. He admonishes us to guard against unwholesome speech; instead we should seek to build others up by what we say (4:29). We should give thanks to God (5:4) and worship Him in the power of the Holy Spirit (5:19–20). Certainly we must pray to the Father, especially when it comes to standing against the devil (6:18). Let's not make excuses that we're too young in the Lord to speak to Him or for Him, because He has given us an adult standing in His family.

Little children can't inherit wealth until they are of age (Gal. 4:1–7), but ever since we experienced spiritual birth, we have been blessed with "every spiritual blessing in Christ" (1:3), and the Spirit guarantees our inheritance (1:14). The riches of His grace have been lavished upon us (1:7–8; 2:7), as well as the riches of His mercy (2:4) and the boundless and glorious riches of Christ (3:8, 16). God's riches in glory can provide our every need, if only we will trust Him (Phil. 4:19). Ishmael was born of the flesh and was a poor slave, but Isaac was born by the power of God and was born wealthy (Gal. 4:21–31).

Babies can't walk. We must carry them until they are big enough and strong enough to stand on their own two feet and walk. Nobody in his right mind would scold a three-month-old child for not playing football! Our old walk was controlled by the world, the flesh and the devil (2:1–3), but our new walk is in God's love and God's light (5:1–14). Instead of following the futile wisdom of this world, we must walk carefully in the wisdom God gives us (5:15–20). We don't have to wait months or years before we can walk in the Spirit (Gal. 5:16–26), because the Spirit's power is available to us the instant we were born again and adopted into God's family.

In Ephesians 6:10–20 Paul didn't write, "Now, when you get older in the Lord, the devil will start attacking you." From the moment we trusted Jesus Christ, we are attacked by Satan and his hosts, because if Satan can't take us to hell, he will try to ruin our Christian walk so that our bad example will send others there in our place. Mothers and fathers protect their little ones, because the children can't protect themselves. But the Lord expects His children to dress themselves in the spiritual armor, take up the sword and shield, pray and defy the Evil One. "Resist the devil, and he will flee from you" (James 4:7).

Since the local church is a family in the Lord, spiritual leaders must be careful to treat the members of the family in love. "Do not rebuke an older man harshly, but exhort him as if he were your father. Treat younger men as brothers, older women as mothers, and younger women as sisters, with absolute purity" (1 Tim. 5:1–2). I have heard some young pastors speak to and about older believers in such unkind ways that the people finally left the church and never returned. If in love older believers offered suggestions or criticisms, the leaders suggested they might want to attend another church. One younger pastor boasted that he had "gotten rid of" the experienced leaders (who were true "elders") and had replaced them with his own young crowd, people who were not leaders but cheerleaders. Now the pastor was "in control."

---

*No family is perfect and no church is perfect, but where you find love and patience, you see church members worshiping and working together.*

---

No family is perfect and no church is perfect, but where you find love and patience, you see church members worshiping and working together. Every human family has members who need to mature and learn how to practice love, and we patiently try to help them all we can. This approach is needed in local churches, and the leaders must set the example. The goal for each member of the church family must be *maturity*. "Then we will no longer be infants, tossed back and forth by the waves, and blown here and there by every wind of teaching and by the cunning and craftiness of people in their deceitful scheming. Instead, speaking the truth in love, we will in all things grow up into him who is the head, that is, Christ" (Eph. 4:14–15).

"Speaking the truth in love" is essential. Truth without love is brutality, and love without truth is hypocrisy; and we don't want either in the church family.

### The body (Eph. 1:22–23; 4:1–16)

The image of the church as a body reminds us that we have a living relationship to Christ, the Head of the body, and also to one another as living members of the same body. Along with Ephesians 4:1–16, Paul deals with "body truth" in First Corinthians 12–14 and Romans 12, making it clear that believers belong to each other, affect each other and need each other. The word "member" doesn't refer primarily to our names on a church roll, as important as that is, but to ourselves as living parts of the body of Christ, indwelt and empowered by the Holy Spirit. Each believer has at least one spiritual gift which must be used "to equip his people for works of service, so that the body of Christ may be built up" (4:12). "For we are . . . to do good works, which God prepared in advance for us to do" (2:10).

When we think of the church as a *family*, we think of *maturity*, but the church as a *body* speaks of *ministry*. In order for Jesus to accomplish His saving work here on earth, He had to have a body. Now that He has returned to heaven, He seeks to accomplish His further work on earth through His body, the church. The church isn't only a building of brick and mortar; it's a living body of people. We regularly go into special buildings called "churches," not as spectators at a performance, but as worshipers of God and as members of the body, and we use our spiritual gifts to edify one another. We call our gatherings "services" because we are there to serve Christ and one another. We are there to edify and to be edified, not to be entertained (4:10–13).

No matter how small the congregation, if the people are truly born again, they belong to His body, "the fullness of him who fills everything in every way" (1:23). It is in this body that God reconciles believing Jews and Gentiles and makes them one in Christ (2:16; 3:6). Christians are part of a spiritual body that is "in heaven and on earth" (3:15), and Jesus Christ is the Head of the body (1:22; 4:15; 5:23). No elected or appointed official on earth has the authority to govern the church of Jesus Christ, for all authority belongs to Jesus Christ (Matt. 28:18–20). As God's people pray, search the Word, exercise their spiritual gifts and yield to the Spirit, the exalted Head is able to work in them and through them to accomplish His purposes.

Each of the "body" passages emphasizes three major themes: unity, diversity and maturity.

|            | Rom. 12   | 1 Cor. 12–14 | Eph. 4:1–16 |
|------------|-----------|--------------|-------------|
| Unity:     | 12:1–5    | 12:1–13      | 4:1–6       |
| Diversity: | 12:6–8    | 12:14–31     | 4:7–13      |
| Maturity:  | 12:9 -21  | 13:1–14:40   | 4:14–16     |

Unity without diversity is uniformity, but diversity without unity is confusion and chaos. It is *maturity* that keeps diversity from destroying unity, and that maturity is evidenced by Christian love. Note that love is the key theme in each of the three "maturity" sections. The human body beautifully illustrates these truths: each of us has one body with many diverse parts that work together as we care for our body in love (5:28–30). The result is that the body matures and ministers (4:14–16). The body of Christ grows by spiritual nutrition, not by mathematical addition, as the Word is preached and taught, as the people pray and as the body "exercises itself" in ministry, not only to one another but also to those outside the fellowship who need to trust Christ.

---

*God's people must be taught to worship, because everything spiritually effective that a local church is and does grows out of worship.*

---

God's people must be taught to worship, because everything spiritually effective that a local church is and does grows out of worship. A worship service that glorifies Jesus Christ, honors the Father and is energized by the Holy Spirit will help to equip God's people for life and service and enable them to walk, witness and work.

A worship service is neither a religious "pep rally" ("C'mon now! Let's all sing!") nor a performance that is rewarded with applause. A true worship service focuses on the Lord, high and lifted up, and everything said and done magnifies God's grace and glory. This kind of church advertises no celebrities. Only God is great.

## *The building (Eph. 2:20–22)*

When Jesus said to His disciples, "I will build my church" (Matt. 16:18–19), He described His church as a building in progress with Himself as the builder. Peter called God's people "living stones" in a "spiritual house" (1 Pet. 2:4–8), and Paul saw the local church as a temple of God that must be built with lasting materials (1 Cor. 3:10–23). One of Paul's favorite words was *edify*—"to build up" (Acts 20:32; Rom. 14:19; 15:2, 20; 1 Cor. 3:9; 8:1; 14:3–5, 12, 17, 26; Eph. 4:12, 16, 29; 1 Thess. 5:11). Both the church universal and the church local are buildings, the temples of the living God (2:20–21; 1 Cor. 3:16–17), and so is the body of each believer (1 Cor. 6:19–20).

If the church as a family points to maturity and as a body points to ministry, then the church as a building points to *glory*, which is one of the major themes of Ephesians. The great goal of redemption is the glory of God (1:6, 12, 14) and our prayer ought to be that He will receive "glory in the church," here on earth today and for all eternity (3:20–21).

The city of Ephesus had the temple of their patron goddess Diana, so the citizens knew something about sacred buildings. But the building Paul refers to relates to the habitations of the true and living God, through the Holy Spirit. Think of it: the church is inhabited by God!

In the Book of Genesis, God "walked" with His people: Adam and Eve (Gen. 3:8), Enoch (Gen. 5:21–24), Noah (Gen. 6:9), and

Abraham, Isaac and Jacob (Gen. 17:1; 24:40; 48:15). But after Israel had been delivered from Egypt, God made a remarkable announcement: He wanted to *dwell* with His people (Exod. 25:1–8). The Lord gave Moses the plans for the tabernacle, the people gave of their substance, and the Holy Spirit gave Bezalel and Oholiab the skill to make the tabernacle and its furnishings (Exod. 31:1–14). Moses dedicated the tabernacle to God, and the glory of God moved in and filled the tabernacle (Exod. 40:34–35).

Other nations had temples, but only Israel had the glory of the true and living God dwelling in their midst (Rom. 9:4)—*and the presence of God's glory was essential to the success of the nation.* It dignified Israel and set them apart from other peoples. It also sanctified them and reminded them to live holy lives and not imitate the sins of their neighbors. "Be holy, for I, the Lord your God, am holy" is found at least eight times in Leviticus alone, and is quoted in First Peter 1:15–16 for God's church today. God's glory unified the nation; at every stopping place in their journey, the tribes pitched their tents around the tabernacle (Num. 2). The glory of God was at the very heart of the camp.

*But there came a day when the glory of God departed from His people!* It was a day when a compromising priesthood, the sons of Eli, "used" their ministry in the tabernacle to satisfy their own lusts (1 Sam. 2:12–4:22). They treated the holy ark of God—His glorious throne where His glory rested—as though it were a religious relic or a good luck charm, but God defeated Israel and gave His ark to the enemy. On that day when everything seemed to fall apart, Eli's daughter-in-law gave birth to a son and named him "Ichabod," which means "the glory has departed" (1 Sam. 4:19–22). Israel had departed from God, so God's glory departed from Israel.

I thank God I've lived through a wonderful era in church history and have had the privilege of hearing and knowing some choice servants of God, but it's also been an era when God's glory has departed from more than one ministry and left that ministry desolate. A new generation came along that "used" gospel ministry to cloak their own hidden agendas, and God simply abandoned them. The machinery kept running, the leaders kept "ministering," the appeal letters kept coming into our mail boxes, and everything was there except the glory of God. You could visit churches where the buildings were impressive and crowded, the musicians were skilled, the "preaching" was entertaining and the applause loud and long, but the glory of God was noticeably absent.

Paul makes it clear that the church's worship must glorify God:

> So if the whole church comes together and everyone speaks in tongues, and inquirers or unbelievers come in, will they not say that you are out of your mind? But if an unbeliever or an inquirer comes in while everyone is prophesying [declaring the Word of God, see 14:1–5], they are convicted of sin and are brought under judgment by all, as the secrets of their hearts are laid bare. So they will fall down and worship God, exclaiming, "God is really among you!" (1 Cor. 14:23–25)

Professional talent, religious oratory, impressive architecture and large crowds of people mean very little to a church *if God is not in our midst to bless*. The newspapers and religious magazines may report the great "success" of such ministries, and encourage other churches to follow their example, but God opens to that church's page in His book and writes "Ichabod" across it—"The glory has departed."

What happened to the tabernacle also happened to the Jewish temple. When Solomon dedicated the temple, God's glory moved in (2 Chron. 7:1–3); but there came a time when that glory moved out. The prophet Ezekiel watched it happen and recorded it in his book:

Now the glory of the God of Israel went up from above the cherubim [in the Holy of holies] where it had been, and moved to the threshold of the temple. . . . Then the glory of the Lord departed from over the threshold of the temple and . . . stopped at the entrance of the east gate of the Lord's house. . . . The glory of the Lord went up from within the city and stopped above the mountain east of it. (Ezek. 9:3; 10:4, 18–19; 11:22)

*Ichabod*—the glory has departed! And why did the glory depart? Ezekiel tells us: the people of Israel were imitating the idolatrous practices of their neighbors *inside the temple of Jehovah!* The religious leaders ignored the Word of the Lord and did whatever pleased the people and brought them to the temple. In Ezekiel's day an unbelieving Gentile visiting the temple would feel right at home and never fall on his face in awe before the glory of the Lord. The glory had departed.

---

*If the church imitates the world and follows the world's wisdom instead of God's Word, how can the church bear witness to a watching world?*

---

God's glory returned to earth in the person of Jesus Christ. "The Word became flesh and made his dwelling [pitched his tent] among us. We have seen his glory" (John 1:14). Jesus also referred to His body as a temple (John 2:19–22). Wicked people abused that temple and nailed it to a cross, but Jesus arose from the dead and returned to heaven in a glorified body. On the Day of Pentecost, He and the Father sent the Holy Spirit, and the glory of God now dwells in His church collectively, in faithful local assemblies (1 Cor. 3:10–23) and in individual believers (6:19–20).

God put Israel into the world to be a "light to the Gentiles," revealing that Jehovah is the true and living God (Isa. 42:6; 49:6), and the church is in the world today to glorify Jesus Christ before all nations. (In Acts 13:46–48, Paul applied these two verses from Isaiah to his own ministry to the Gentiles.) The Holy Spirit enables us to glorify Jesus before a needy world: "He [the Spirit] will glorify me," said Jesus (John 16:14). But if the church imitates the world and follows the world's wisdom instead of God's Word, how can the church bear witness to a watching world? The fact that Christians are *different* is what attracts the world. "In the same way, let your light shine before others, that they may see your good deeds and glorify your Father in heaven" (Matt. 5:16).

I want to focus on Paul's words in First Corinthians 3:10–23. He isn't writing here about Christians building their own lives—although you can make that application—but about Christians building the local church. The Corinthian church was making the mistake many church leaders are making today: following human "wisdom" and not God's divine wisdom in building the church. The foundation of the local church is Jesus Christ, and He is the *only* foundation. To build a church on anything or anyone else means that the church will not glorify God—nor will it last.

The wisdom of this world is but "wood, hay or straw," cheap temporary materials that you can pick up without much effort on the surface of the earth, but the wisdom of God is like "gold, silver, costly stones," lasting materials that we must dig for because they are buried deep in God's Word (Prov. 2:1–10; 3:13–15; 8:8–11). *If we want to build with lasting materials, we must dig into the Holy Scriptures!* To "borrow" the world's ideas and methods instead of using the Scriptures is to build with materials that will not last. The novelist George MacDonald wrote,

"In whatever man does without God, he must fail miserably, or succeed miserably."

What a disgrace it is to the ministry when a church discovers that the pastor is plagiarizing messages instead of taking time to dig into the Word. How many preachers attend conferences, not to receive blessing for their own hearts, but to get sermon outlines to carry them through another season? Years ago, a veteran preacher gave me good advice: "Study hard and milk a lot of cows, *but make your own butter!*" The saintly Scottish preacher Robert Murray M'Cheyne used to say of his sermon preparation, "Oil—beaten oil for the sanctuary," referring to Exodus 27:20–21 and Leviticus 24:1–4 in the King James. *Beaten* oil, not stolen oil.

Paul calls the church "a holy temple in the Lord" and reminds us that we "are being built together to become a dwelling in which God lives by his Spirit" (Eph. 2:21–22). But just as God removed the glory from the tabernacle and the temple, so He can remove the lampstand from any church that follows the world's wisdom and ceases to love Christ and glorify Him. That was His warning to the Ephesian church, the church that had forsaken their first love (Rev. 2:4–5). The word "love" is used in one form or another at least twenty-four times in the Ephesian letter, and Paul closed the letter with "Grace to all who love our Lord Jesus Christ with an undying love" (Eph. 6:24).

But the Ephesian saints didn't heed the warning. In spite of their orthodoxy, hard work, busy activities and personal sacrifices, they allowed their "first-love flame" to die out. Without love for Jesus, their ministry was only so much religious activity. God removed their lampstand and the light of their witness was gone. The believers still assembled regularly and went through the motions of worshiping and serving the Lord, but it meant little and accomplished nothing. "Ichabod—the glory has departed."

## *The flock (Eph. 4:11)*

"Christ himself gave [to the church] . . . pastors and teachers . . . ." The word "pastor" comes from the Latin and means "shepherd." The root word is *pasco*, which means "to feed." The fact that Paul connects "pastors" and "teachers" indicates that the shepherd feeds the sheep by leading them into "the green pastures and still waters" of the Word of God. After His resurrection Jesus made Peter the fisherman into Peter the shepherd and gave him three commands: "Feed my lambs . . . Take care of my sheep . . . Feed my sheep" (John 21:15–17). Years later, Peter wrote to the elders of the churches in the Roman provinces, "Be shepherds of God's flock that is under your care, watching over them—not because you must, but because you are willing, as God wants you to be" (1 Pet. 5:2).

We dealt with the "flock" image in Paul's address to the Ephesian elders, but there are a few other matters I would like to share.

Frequently in the Old Testament, God's people Israel are compared to a flock and the Lord to their shepherd: "we are his people, the sheep of his pasture" (Ps. 100:3). Moses feared that, without godly leadership, the people of Israel would become "like sheep without a shepherd" (Num. 27:17), and unfortunately that's exactly what happened (Ezek. 34). Their leaders exploited the sheep instead of caring for them and eventually led the nation into destruction and the people into captivity. Everything rises or falls with leadership, and a shepherd must lead.

We may think that the Lord is unkind because He compares His people to sheep, but He knows us better than we do and is only being honest. At the same time He is also comparing Himself to a shepherd, and in New Testament times shepherding was a despised occupation. A person who wanted to achieve greatness and recognition would never become a shepherd, because it was a lonely, despised and dangerous calling. Even though great men like Abraham, Isaac, Jacob, Joseph and David were shepherds, pious Jews in New Testament times refused to do business with shepherds. They put shepherds into the same category as thieves and wouldn't even allow them to give witness in court. (Interestingly, God turned this social stigma on its ear when He used shepherds to give the first witness of the birth of Jesus!)

---

*If you try to drive sheep, you will only scatter them. The shepherd goes before the sheep and they follow him.*

---

But God's people are like sheep whether we like it or not, and those who lead them must be faithful shepherds with a heart for the flock. Like sheep, we are relatively defenseless and prone to wander, and the shepherd must frequently go and search for sheep that have strayed. Like sheep, we flock together and care for one another, and we must be profitable to the shepherd. In Bible times sheep were kept primarily for wool and milk and for breeding, and they were killed only when sacrificed at the sanctuary or slaughtered for special occasions of feasting.

Sheep that lack a faithful shepherd may become ill, develop infections from wounds or wander off and become the prey of every predator. Sheep need constant care, and the shepherd must go before them to make sure the pasture has no dangers, such as hidden holes, snakes or sharp rocks. The faithful shepherd was a combination of guide, protector, physician and provider, and he was on the job day and night.

If you try to drive sheep, you will only scatter them. The shepherd goes *before* the sheep and they follow him. Each sheep had a name and could recognize the shepherd's voice when that name was called (John 10:1–14). "Don't let anyone look down on you because you are young," Paul advised Timothy, "but set an example for the believers in speech, in conduct, in love, in faith and in purity" (1 Tim. 4:12). He told Titus, "In everything set them an example by doing what is good" (Titus 2:7). A bad example can undo the impact of a good sermon.

Of course, Jesus is the "good shepherd" who died for the sheep (John 10:11–18), the "great shepherd" who equips the sheep for service (Heb. 13:20–21) and the "chief shepherd" who, when He returns, will reward the faithful shepherds for their good work (1 Pet. 5:1–4). We are never more like Jesus than when we love His sheep and minister to them.

## *Marriage (Eph. 5:22–33)*

Paul admonished the Ephesian believers to "be filled with the Spirit" (5:18) and gave the evidences of this fullness: Spirit-controlled saints are joyful (5:19), thankful (5:20) and submissive (5:21). He then applied this principle to marriage (5:22–33), raising a family (6:1–4) and doing our jobs in the marketplace (6:5–9). It's one thing to praise God in church with "psalms, hymns and songs from the Spirit" (5:19) and quite something else to control our anger and joyfully submit to others at home and at work.

But Paul reached beyond this valuable practical counsel and pointed out that Christian marriage is a picture of the relationship between Christ and the church. Four times in this section Paul tells the Christian husbands to love their wives, and three times he tells the wives to submit to their husbands. But note in verse 21 that he tells *all the saints* to submit to one another in the Lord. We are members of Christ's body in a living relationship, and we are "married to Christ" in a loving relationship that must "spill over" to others. "God's love has been poured out into our hearts through the Holy Spirit who has been given to us" (Rom. 5:5).

Submission is not subjugation or slavery. Submission is finding our true freedom in Christ by willingly and lovingly serving
others with the gifts He has given us. When Christ is our Master,
we have no problem serving others, for He is our example and
our enablement. No wife hesitates to submit to a loving, submissive husband, and no husband has a problem yielding to a
loving, submissive wife. The first word in "wedding" is "we," for
in marriage two become one and the words "mine" and "yours"
are joyfully replaced by "ours."

But back to the church at Ephesus and to local churches
today. Jesus revealed that the basic problem in the Ephesian congregation was that they had forsaken their first love for Christ
(Rev. 2:4). Yes, they were a busy church and an orthodox church,
and any visitor would have given them high marks; but Jesus
saw things differently and threatened to remove their lampstand.
When Jesus restored Peter to discipleship, His repeated question
was, "Do you love me?" (John 21:15–19), for if we truly love
Jesus, that will take care of every aspect of the Christian life.
"Anyone who loves me will obey my teaching" (John 14:23).

Paul connected Christian worship with our being filled with
the Spirit and expressing our love for the Lord (5:18–20). There
was a time when a worship service opened with an invocation,
and we asked the Lord to help us to worship "in the Spirit and
in truth" (John 4:23); but invocations have disappeared along
with benedictions ("So long, folks! Thanks for coming!"). As for
worship that expresses love to Jesus, that too is fading away and
giving place to songs about "I," "me," "my" and "mine." The juvenile lyrics of many so-called "praise choruses" must grieve the
Holy Spirit as He longs to point us to Jesus and glorify Him.

Worshipers and worship leaders must be filled not only with
the Spirit of God but also with the Word of God. "Let the message of Christ dwell among you richly as you teach and admon-

ish one another with all wisdom through psalms, hymns, and songs from the Spirit, singing to God with gratitude in your hearts" (Col. 3:16–17). As with the fullness of the Spirit, believers filled with the Word are joyful, thankful and submissive, because the Holy Spirit works in them through the Word.

---

*What does the Lord think of churches today that worship statistics, imitate the world, and ignore prayer, the Word and the Holy Spirit?*

---

This explains why Paul admonished Timothy, "Until I come, devote yourself to the public reading of Scripture, to preaching and to teaching" (1 Tim. 4:13). It appears that all three of these essential ministries are on the way out. The pastor's sermon text (if he has one) is usually read publicly, but the ancient practice of reading from the law, the prophets, the gospels and the epistles is maintained today primarily by what the "independent" believers call "the liturgical churches." (Every church has a liturgy, either a good one or a bad one. A liturgy that disobeys Paul is a bad one.) As for teaching the Word, many "sermons" are shallow and cleverly entertaining, lacking authority and rarely pointing to Christ. I have heard more than one preacher in an orthodox church who in thirty minutes never once mentioned Jesus. Shame on us!

Is it any wonder that "church worship" has become entertainment, "fun" and "feeling good about ourselves"? A congregation that isn't filled with the Spirit of God and doesn't know the Word of God is incapable of worshiping God "in the Spirit and in truth [the Word]" (John 4:24). *Christian worship is a serious activity, and we cannot compensate for our spiritual poverty by loud applause, flashing colored lights or increased decibels.* The God we worship sees our hearts, and the Spirit longs to deepen our worship experience.

Under the old covenant the nation of Israel was called "the wife of Yahweh" (Isa. 54:5–6; Jer. 2–3; 13:20–27; Ezek. 16; Hosea), and God called her repeated idolatry "prostitution." What does the Lord think of churches today that worship statistics, imitate the world and ignore prayer, the Word and the Holy Spirit? Perhaps James 4:4 is the answer: "You adulterous people, don't you know that friendship with the world means enmity against God? Anyone who chooses to be a friend of the world becomes an enemy of God."

James has a remedy: "Submit yourselves, then, to God. Resist the devil, and he will flee from you. Come near to God and he will come near to you. Wash your hands, you sinners, and purify your hearts, you double-minded" (4:7–8).

Many religious systems have no songs, but our Christian faith is a "singing" faith. Moses taught the Jewish nation a song before he left them (Deut. 32), and Deborah the judge sang after a great victory (Judges 5). David and other singers left us the psalms. Paul and Silas sang in the Philippian *prison* (Acts 16:16–40), and there are songs in the Gospels, the Epistles and the Apocalypse. Why? *Because our God sings!* God the Father rejoices over His people with singing (Zeph. 3:17); God the Son sang at the Passover feast (Matt. 26:30) and after His resurrection (Ps. 22:22ff; Heb. 2:12); *and God the Holy Spirit sings through the church today if we are worshiping as God wants us to worship* (Eph. 5:18–20).

Do those who plan worship services take time to consult the Spirit and the Word to determine what ought to be sung? What a tragedy it is when the church of Jesus Christ week after week grieves the Holy Spirit in the most important ministry of the church—the worship of the true and living God. Does the Holy

Spirit enjoy and want to bless our juvenile lyrics, our mindless repetitions and our shallow imitations of the of the entertainment world?

Paul brought marriage and worship together in Ephesians 5:21–33 because true worship is an expression of our love to the Lord. In the traditional *Book of Common Prayer*, the marriage ceremony includes the statement, "With this ring I thee wed, with my body I thee worship, and with all my worldly goods I thee endow." We truly love Jesus Christ because we are joined to Him as in marriage (Rom. 7:1–4; Eph. 5:21–33), and so we give Him our body (Rom. 12:1–2) and our worldly goods, and we tell Him in our worship that we love Him. Worship is not entertainment; it's an act of endearment that's as serious as marriage.

The problem is, marriage isn't serious anymore. It's "for better or for worse, but not for long." As church worship services have become more casual and entertainment-oriented, I've noted that weddings and funerals are following suit, introducing practices unworthy of the Christian faith.

It's all part of the same sin: we grieve the Holy Spirit, He can't bless us, and so we have to invent clever new practices to compensate for His absence. As long as the audience is pleased and goes away feeling good, it doesn't bother us that God may be displeased and has written "Ichabod" over the church—"the glory has departed."

No sooner had Moses and Aaron dedicated the tabernacle and the priesthood than Nadab and Abihu, Aaron's sons, tried to rush into the building with censers containing "unauthorized fire," and the Lord killed them (Lev. 10:1–12). The admonition in Leviticus 10:8 suggests that the young men had enjoyed too much wine, which ties the event to Paul's warning in Ephesians 5:18: "Do not get drunk on wine."

For every God-given spiritual blessing, the world and the

devil have a counterfeit, and wine is the world's substitute for the fullness of the Spirit. Nadab and Abihu didn't take the fire from off the altar, the fire God had sent from heaven (Lev. 9:22–24), but from some other source. If today the Lord killed every preacher and worship leader who "ministered" in the strength of carnal substitutes, would any of us still be alive?

Wicked King Ahaz saw an attractive pagan altar in Damascus and ordered that one just like it be constructed for the temple in Jerusalem (1 Kings 16:10–20)—*and nobody opposed him!* In fact, the high priest supervised the construction of the altar. Everybody ignored the word of the Lord to Moses: "Make this tabernacle and all its furnishings exactly like the pattern I will show you" (Exod. 25:9, 40; 26:30; 27:8; Acts 7:44), a command quoted in the New Testament (Heb. 8:5). How many pagan altars has the church copied and dragged into the sanctuary, yet God in His grace withholds His judgment, and we interpret His longsuffering as divine approval. After all, the people keep coming! But does the Lord come to our meetings and bless us?

---

*Everything the local church is, says and does depends on worship. If our worship is wrong, very little else will be right.*

---

Over thirty years ago Francis Schaeffer said this about apostasy: "In church history, a cycle seems to recur: Living orthodoxy moves to dead orthodoxy and then to heterodoxy."[6] This pattern may also apply to congregational worship. First there is *living worship*—in the Spirit, obedient to the Word, backed by prayer and from the heart of the worshipers. Then comes *dead worship*—a dull routine that lacks the power of the Spirit and doesn't come from the heart. Finally, there is *false worship*—an attempt to rekindle the lost fire with what turns out to be false fire. Enthusiasm and entertainment replace enlightenment and spiritual enrichment.

Everything the local church is, says and does depends on worship. If our worship is wrong, very little else will be right. If we try to improve church programs and promotion but don't improve our worship, we only make matters worse. "These are the ones I look on with favor: those who are humble and contrite in spirit and who tremble at my word" (Isa. 66:2).

The greatest of all God's commandments is "Love the Lord your God with all your heart and with all your soul and with all your mind" (Matt. 22:34–38). Worship is the church's highest privilege and greatest responsibility because it expresses our love and devotion to the Lord. This means that careless worship is the committing of the greatest sin, for we are not bringing God our very best.

## *The army (Eph. 6:12–20)*

Unless we watch our "spiritual posture," we will fail as soldiers. We must know where we are seated (Eph. 2:4), how to kneel and pray (3:14), how to walk in obedience to the Lord (4:1, 17; 5:2, 8, 15), and how to be filled with the Spirit and submit to God and to others (5:15–20). If we fail in these "spiritual postures," we will never be able to take our stand against the devil and defeat him (6:10–20). That may be why Paul left this admonition to the very end of his letter, for all he wrote before is preparation for the battle. As we saw in our survey of Acts, Satan first comes as the lion to devour, and if that fails, he gets into the church as the serpent that deceives. But he has a host of demonic forces that Paul identifies as "the spiritual forces of evil in the heavenly realms" (6:12), and it is against these that we must fight.

I don't believe that demons can inhabit the temple of God

where God's Holy Spirit dwells, but demonic forces can influence the minds and hearts of God's people and lead them into sin. A lying spirit enticed David to take a census of Israel, and this led to the death of 70,000 people (1 Chron. 21). When we believe God's truth, the Holy Spirit works in us, but when we accept a Satanic lie as God's truth, then Satan goes to work in and through us. This is what happened to Peter (Matt. 16:21–23), to Ananias and Sapphira (Acts 5:1–11), and to the leaders of the church in Corinth (2 Cor. 11:1–4). It's possible for sincere Christians to believe they are filled with the Spirit when actually they are being fooled by the spirits.

Paul's admonition "put on the armor of light" is followed by "clothe yourselves with the Lord Jesus Christ" (Rom. 13:12, 14), which suggests that the pieces of the spiritual armor speak of the attributes and character of our Savior. The belt of truth speaks of integrity (6:14), and Jesus is the truth (John 14:6). The breastplate of righteousness (6:14) signifies the imputed righteousness of Christ, who is our righteousness (1 Cor. 1:30; 2 Cor. 5:21). The shoes of peace point to Christ our peace (Eph. 2:14) and the shield of faith tells of Jesus who is called "Faithful and True" (Rev. 19:11). As for the helmet of salvation, old Simeon looked at the child Jesus and exclaimed, "For my eyes have seen your salvation" (Luke 2:30). The sword of the Spirit is the Word of God, and so is our Savior (John 1:1, 14; Rev. 19:13).

To wear the armor is to be clothed with Jesus Christ. An old gospel song puts it this way:

> Stand up, stand up for Jesus; stand on His strength alone.
> The arm of flesh will fail you—You dare not trust your own.
> Put on the gospel armor—Each piece put on with prayer.
> Where duty calls or danger, be never wanting there.[7]

We are protected by God's truth, righteousness, peace, faithfulness and salvation, and we can attack the Enemy with the

Word of God (Heb. 4:12). Even more, the power for battle that we need comes from prayer and yielding to the Holy Spirit. "Reflect on what I am saying, for the Lord will give you insight into all this" (2 Tim. 2:7). There are over fifty references to the Holy Spirit in the Book of Acts and at least twenty-five references to prayer. Are we such superior Christians today that we can do without these essentials?

---

*So many of God's "soldiers" are AWOL and not wearing their armor.*

---

The unfortunate thing is that so many of God's "soldiers" are AWOL and not wearing their armor, so that the church of Jesus Christ is a pitiful army. Furthermore, too many of the soldiers are fighting each other instead of attacking the real Enemy, Satan (Eph. 6:11–12). The "soldier saints" lack discipline and pay very little attention to their Commander's orders. Five times in his first letter to Timothy, the apostle Paul uses the Greek word *parangello,* which means "a military command, instructions from headquarters." With this in mind, read First Timothy 1:3, 4:11, 5:7, and 6:13 and 17. The Lord doesn't give us instructions and beg us to obey. When He gives orders, He expects us to obey; and often He must ask, "Why do you call me 'Lord, Lord,' and do not do what I say?" (Luke 6:46). Why, indeed?

Of what practical value in our daily lives and ministries are these images of the local church?

For one thing, they tell us what we believers are in God's sight and how we relate to Him, to each other and to the world around us. Understanding these images encourages us to find our proper place in the church and to do our job faithfully for His glory. Not to know my spiritual gift, or to know it and not use it in His service, is the equivalent of working for the enemy—and in the armed forces this is known as *treason*. Officers don't make suggestions; they give orders, and Jesus is the Commander-in-Chief.

These images also remind us that each believer and each local church is important to the Lord. When preaching to pastors, I've often said, "There are no small churches and there are no big preachers." The media people puff the big churches and the popular preachers because many people in the Christian public equate size and position with success, but God isn't always impressed with the things that impress the public. "Jesus said, "What people value highly is detestable in God's sight" (Luke 16:15). Evangelist D.L. Moody used to say, "Converts should be weighed as well as counted," and the same principle applies to local congregations.

I've found these images helpful in facing and solving church problems. Some problems are "family problems" and will be solved when people mature in the Lord (4:14), so God's servants must patiently keep loving the saints, feeding them the Word and praying for them. Other problems are "body problems" because people don't know their spiritual gifts and therefore are "square pegs in round holes." We must help them discover and develop their spiritual gifts and find the right places where they are to serve the Lord. When the church is experiencing a crisis, we may have to view the congregation as an army and ourselves as God's officers, and handle the emergency with loving authority. But to become a general when what the church needs is a gentle shepherd is only to make the problem worse. Sheep are led, not driven.

Another value from the Ephesian letter is Paul's emphasis on God's great purpose to bring everything together in Jesus Christ (1:10). The church isn't expected to manufacture unity in the body of Christ but to maintain the unity that God has already created (4:1–6). If we would get rid of our cheap imitations of the world, use our spiritual gifts and draw upon the riches of our fullness in Christ, there would be more unity in the church, and we would make a greater impact in today's shattered world (4:11–16).

---

*The job is too great for us and only the Head of the church, Jesus Christ, can help us faithfully do our work.*

---

Finally, recognizing the many images of the church reminds us that the job is too great for us and only the Head of the church, Jesus Christ, can help us faithfully do our work. He is the vine and His people are the branches, and without Him we can do nothing (John 15:5). We aren't merely handicapped; we are paralyzed. He is the Chief Shepherd, and we are under-shepherds who follow Him. He is also the "commander of the army of the Lord" (Josh. 5:13–15), and we are second in command. We need to remember that. It will help to keep us humble.

Why do we get upset when we learn about sinners acting like sinners? After all, that's their nature. We ought to be upset when *saints* act like sinners, because we are God's children and possess a divine nature (2 Pet. 1:3–5). Judgment begins in God's household, especially when we have turned it into religious business (1 Pet. 4:17; Matt. 21:12–13). When I was teaching pastors in seminary graduate programs, I urged them to preach messages explaining and applying the biblical images of the church. If we Christians don't know who and what we are in Jesus Christ, how can we live and serve the way God wants us to? D.L. Moody didn't permit Ira Sankey to use the song "Onward Christian Soldiers" in their evangelistic services, because Moody said that the church was too unlike an army to sing about it. He should see churches today.

Obviously, there is much more that can be said about the Ephesian doctrine of the church, but we must move on. I suggest you study the many references to the Holy Spirit and to prayer in this profound letter, and pay special attention to Paul's two significant prayers (1:15–23; 3:14–21). Frequently read through Ephesians using different translations and saturate your soul with its teachings. Let's not be like those professed Christians in Ephesus whose spiritual knowledge was incomplete (Acts 18:24–28) and whose spiritual experience was inadequate (Acts 19:1–7).

# 6

# The Ephesian Emphasis, Part 3

IN HIS SERMON "Timothy as a Young Minister," Alexander Whyte quotes John Calvin as saying, "What I owe to these two epistles to Timothy can never be told." Whether we are old or young in the ministry, Calvin's words ought to be recommendation enough for us to take time to consider what Paul wrote in these two pastoral letters. There's a great deal of preaching these days, but pastoral ministry seems to be neglected if not forgotten.

Timothy was Paul's official apostolic representative to the churches in Roman Asia that Paul had planted during three years' ministry in Ephesus. Paul's emphasis in these letters is "how people ought to conduct themselves in God's household, which is the church of the living God, the pillar and the foundation of the truth" (1 Tim. 3:15).

As we read these letters, we sense that Timothy felt totally inadequate to succeed the great apostle and that he probably wanted to minister somewhere else. After the greeting in the first letter, Paul's first words are "stay there in Ephesus" (1:3). Three times in my ministry I have succeeded well-known and greatly gifted men whose ministries were effective and extensive, so I can identify with young Timothy's concerns. Paul's counsel to Timothy can encourage all of God's servants today: "But you, keep your head in all situations, endure hardship, do the work of an evangelist, discharge all the duties of your ministry" (2 Tim. 4:5). That says it all.

---

*Everything the church does rises and falls with leadership.*

---

Let's consider some of the topics Paul emphasizes in this correspondence.

*Leadership.* I pointed out in the last chapter Paul's repeated use of the Greek word *parangello* in First Timothy, usually translated "command, charge, instruct." It refers to a military command that must be obeyed (1:3; 4:11; 5:7; 6:13, 17). In these days of "individual Christianity," when people meet in small groups and exchange their ignorance of the Bible ("Well, that's what the verse says to me!"), this word "command" isn't too popular.

As I have said before, everything the church does rises and falls with leadership—committed leadership, biblically-trained leadership, praying leadership, sacrificing leadership, Spirit-empowered leadership. If Timothy didn't lead the church, somebody else would, and then the body would be divided and the ministry would be weakened. There were already false teachers invading the churches (1 Tim. 1:3–7), and Timothy had to deal with the Enemy courageously. He was to "take care of" God's church just as a father would "manage" a family (1 Tim. 3:4–5; 5:17). The word translated "take care of" literally means "to stand before." The NIV translates it "leadership" in Rom. 12:8.

Timothy lived in a culture that worshiped status and authority. Wherever you looked, you saw Roman officials and Roman soldiers, and the Romans were known for their ability to take charge. However, Timothy wasn't to follow their example but the example of Jesus. Our Lord's disciples occasionally were guilty of arguing over who was the greatest among them, and Jesus made it clear that He was their example and not the Gentiles who "exercised lordship" over people (Luke 22:24–27). God's leaders are the people's servants, and only God is great.

A wealth of information on "leadership" is available today, and we must be careful to test what the experts say by what the Bible says. It's simple for a writer to borrow the world's ideas of leadership, drop in a few Bible verses and give the impression that this counsel is indeed the will of God. But God's ways and thoughts are light-years higher than ours (Isa. 55:8–9), and the Bible records the sad consequences of well-meaning leaders who abandoned God's way of doing things for their own clever ideas.

Moses struck the rock instead of speaking to it and was banned from Canaan (Num. 20:1–13). Twice Joshua made decisions without consulting God and ended up being defeated by the enemy (Joshua 7) and then having to defend the enemy (Joshua 9). David bypassed the Levites and had the ark of God carried to Jerusalem on a cart, much to his embarrassment (2 Sam. 6). In deciding whether or not to leave port, Julius the Roman centurion listened to the "experts" instead of to Paul, took a vote and had the majority with him, and ended up wrecking the ship (Acts 27). George MacDonald was right: "In whatever man does without God, he must fail miserably or succeed more miserably."

*Teaching.* Another major emphasis in these two epistles is *the importance of teaching the Word of God to God's people.* (See 1 Tim. 2:7, 12; 3:2; 4:11; 6:2; 2 Tim. 1:11; 2:2, 24; 4:2–3.) God had given His Word to Paul (1 Tim. 1:11), who in turn gave it to Timothy (1:18–19), who was commanded to guard it (1 Tim. 6:20; 2 Tim. 1:13–14) and pass it on to others (2 Tim. 2:2). Each local church is one generation short of extinction, so each new generation of believers must be taught what Paul called "the faith" (1 Tim. 1:19; 3:9; 4:1).

During more than fifty years of ministry, I've seen many false teachings attempt to influence the Christian church, and the battles have been intense; but the church and the faith are still here, thanks to obedient Christians who pass on God's truth. Topical sermons may have their place, but they can never substitute for the verse-by-verse exposition of the Scriptures, where the preacher explains and applies God's truth. Topical preaching may attract a curious crowd, but it's not likely to build a strong church.

While on this subject, we must note Paul's emphasis on "sound teaching" (1 Tim. 1:10, 6:3; 2 Tim. 1:13, 4:3). The Greek word translated "sound" gives us the English word "hygiene" and means "healthy." Sound doctrine is healthy doctrine that produces strong, well-balanced Christians. False doctrine is "sick" doctrine and "will spread like gangrene" (2 Tim. 2:17–18) in the church. God's Word is the healthy food we need for growth and strength (Matt. 4:4; 1 Tim. 4:6; 1 Pet. 2:2; 1 Cor. 3:1–2), the water we need for keeping clean (Ps. 119:9; Eph. 5:26–27) and the medicine we require when we find ourselves infected (Ps. 107:20).

*Godliness.* Paul is careful to tell Timothy and the other church leaders to make a priority of *maintaining their own spiritual walk.* "Have nothing to do with godless myths and old wives' tales;

rather, train yourself to be godly. For physical training is of some value, but godliness has value for all things, holding promise for both the present life and the life to come" (1 Tim. 4:7–8).

The word translated "train" gives us the English word "gymnasium." Not unlike society today, both the Greeks and the Romans in New Testament times were caught up in physical culture and competitive sports. Knowing this, Paul told the church leaders to put as much effort into their personal spiritual development as they did their physical development. I've known church leaders who put far more time and money into their golf game than their Bible study or prayer life, and the churches suffered.

The goal Paul set for the minister is a godly life (1 Tim. 6:11) that is devoted to a pastoral ministry which builds a congregation known for godliness (1 Tim. 1:5, 2:2; 6:3–6). This is a godliness that comes from the victory of Jesus Christ on the cross and His present ministry in heaven (1 Tim. 3:16).

Neither the minister nor the congregation wants the reputation of "having a form of godliness but denying its power" (2 Tim. 3:5), what G. Campbell Morgan called "reputation without reality." Paul admonished Timothy to "fan into flame the gift of God" he had received when Paul laid hands on him, probably at his ordination (2 Tim. 1:6). Early each morning, the Old Testament priests began their day at the altar, adding fuel to the fire and getting it ready for the sacrifices the people would bring (Lev. 6:12–13). That's a good example for us to follow.

We used to sing a song that said, "Give of your best to the Master." Paul had that theme in mind when he told Timothy to work hard in his ministry, to exercise discipline and give his very best to the Lord's work. "Be diligent in these matters; give yourself wholly to them, so that everyone may see your progress. Watch your life and doctrine closely. Persevere in them, for if you do, you will save both yourself and your hearers" (1 Tim. 4:15–16).

The word "progress" means "pioneer advance." It describes the minister who isn't stuck on a comfortable treadmill but leads the church family into new experiences of grace and new opportunities of service. Paul used verbs like "labor" and "strive" to describe the Christian ministry (1 Tim. 4:10). "Work hard and agonize" are good synonyms, and "the hardworking farmer" is a good illustration of what the Christian ministry is all about (2 Tim. 2:6). The esteemed Scottish preacher Alexander Whyte said, "I would have laziness held to be the one unpardonable sin in all our students and in all our ministers."[8]

---

*Paul used verbs like "labor" and "strive" to describe the Christian ministry.*

---

Younger ministers are wise to ask the Lord to lead them to experienced servants of God in their area who can mentor and encourage them. I personally thank God for the veterans who counseled me, encouraged me and prayed for me in my early days as a pastor. Too many new ministers would rather "hang out" with their peers and drink coffee than to sit at the feet of a battle-scarred veteran and learn how to serve, although both are important and necessary. "It is the malady of our age," wrote Eric Hoffer, "that the young are so busy teaching us that they have no time left to learn."[9]

The generations need each other. Younger ministers help me catch up on the present, and in return, I help them catch up on the past. If we don't reopen the "old wells," as Isaac did (Gen. 26:18), and drink the water that sustained previous generations, we will end up accepting cheap substitutes and missing the blessing that our Lord promised in John 7:37–39.

Timothy was called, not just to preach the faith, but also

to *live on* the faith, "nourished on the truths of the faith and upon the good teaching" that he had heard from Paul (1 Tim. 4:6). This meant diligently devoting himself to reading, studying, meditating and praying, asking God's help so he could "set an example for the believers in speech, in conduct, in love, in faith and in purity" (1 Tim. 4:12). The lives that we live are more important than the sermons that we preach, because people who aren't reading their Bibles are reading our lives, and those who do read their Bibles want us to obey what God says. The best way to prove that Jesus is alive is for us to live like Jesus and let our light shine. It's good to be a studious expositor, but it's also good to be a sanctified example.

*Integrity.* Five times in his epistles to Timothy, Paul wrote about the conscience of the Christian believer. Conscience is the window in the heart that lets God's light shine in so we can know God's will, make right decisions and build character. God requires us to cultivate a good conscience (1 Tim. 1:5, 19) and a clear conscience (1 Tim. 3:9; 2 Tim. 1:3) so the "window" isn't dirty. When the conscience is defiled, then the light becomes darkness (Luke 11:34–36). If we sin against God's light, we're in danger of developing a "seared" conscience (1 Tim. 4:2) that doesn't function at all. We weep when we hear about servants of God whose secret sins become public scandals and disgrace the gospel and the ministry. When believers allow the dirt to accumulate on the window pane, it blots out the light of God's truth and they stop "walking in the light" (1 John 1:5–10). We must beware when we get accustomed to inner darkness (1 John 1:7).

*Love.* Paul uses the familiar word *agape* (sacrificing love) nine times in his letters to Timothy, because apart from God's love, there can be no effective ministry (1 Tim. 1:5). Paul had experienced that love (1 Tim. 1:14) and so has every true believer (Rom. 5:8); and if we walk in the Spirit, the fragrant fruit of

God's love will be evident (Gal. 5:22–26). God's shepherds must not only be examples of love (1 Tim. 4:14) but must diligently pursue it (1 Tim. 6:11; 2 Tim. 2:22).

Christian love simply means that we treat others just as God treats us, and the Holy Spirit gives us the enablement we need. "For the Spirit God gave us does not make us timid, but he gives us power, love and self-discipline" (2 Tim. 1:7). *We should love God's people through God's Word* (2 Tim. 1:13). To hide behind a pulpit and shoot at the sheep is not the biblical pattern for ministry. In your reading and your friendships, get acquainted with authors and preachers who speak the truth in love, and learn from them, just as Timothy learned from Paul (2 Tim. 3:10).

In the third of his classic *Yale Lectures on Preaching*, "The Preacher in His Work," Phillips Brooks says it best. He maintains that the preacher must be a pastor to have sympathy and be able to preach to real people, while the pastor must be a preacher so that he might have authority from the Word to lead the flock into God's will. The preacher who divorces what God has married will lack either authority or sympathy and have a difficult time either winning his congregation's hearts or motivating their wills. Balanced shepherds develop balanced sheep.

*Truth.* Paul mentions truth at least a dozen times in these epistles. He commands Timothy to beware of false doctrine and to expose it and those who teach it. To be saved means to "come to the knowledge of the truth," and that truth is found in Jesus (1 Tim. 2:1–5; 4:3). To believe in Jesus is to become part of "the church of the living God, the pillar and foundation of the truth" (1 Tim. 3:15). To believe lies is to be "robbed of the truth" (1 Tim. 6:1–5), to wander away from the truth (2 Tim. 2:18), to stop listening to the truth (2 Tim. 4:4) and to oppose the truth (2 Tim. 3:8). The Scriptures are "the word of truth" and must be handled correctly (2 Tim. 2:15). There is no middle ground.

While there are always new insights and applications to be found in the Scriptures, there is no new "word of God." False teachers are not instructed by the Holy Spirit but by their own inflated egos and seducing spirits (1 Tim. 1:6–7 and 6:4; 1 Tim. 4:1–3; 2 Tim. 3:6, 8, 13; 4:3–4). Timothy must handle such doctrines like a chemist handles poisons: he must know what they are but never allow them to get into his system. "Have nothing to do with such people" (2 Tim. 3:5). However, some church members err because of ignorance or immaturity, so we must exercise discernment and patiently try to help them (2 Tim. 2:23–26).

---

*Anything we do in the name of Jesus that helps people and involves personal sacrifice is Christian service.*

---

*Service.* But Paul did more than sound the alarm about false teaching; he also told Timothy to encourage his people to let their light shine and do good deeds to the glory of God. Here he was only repeating what Jesus had taught (Matt. 5:13–15) and what the apostolic church had practiced (Acts 2:42–47; see James 2:14–26). Paul specifically mentions the women (1 Tim. 2:9–15; 5:9–10), but all believers were expected to devote themselves to good works. We are prepared vessels "to do any good work" (2 Tim. 2:21). The mark of a true Bible student isn't a big head but a busy life, service to the Lord and to people in need (2 Tim. 3:16–17).

The term "full-time Christian service" can be misleading. "Full-time Christian *living*" is what Paul is writing about, and that involves service by the entire church, not just the elders. But serving Jesus involves much more than singing in the choir, attending board meetings, playing an instrument or even preaching a sermon, as good and necessary as those activities are. Anything we do in the name of Jesus that helps people and involves personal sacrifice is Christian service (Phil. 2:14–18) and will be rewarded, and that includes even giving a cup of cold water to a stranger (Matt. 10:42).

For years I've urged youth pastors to ask the local authorities what volunteer work could be done for the city, and then put their teens and collegians to work right at home; but alas, I've had very little success. Let there be a catastrophe and people will join the crowd of helpers, and this is good; but why must the routine but important tasks that keep society moving be ignored?

Ephesians 4:11–12 tells us that all the saints are involved in the "works of service." The congregation doesn't pay the elders and staff to do their work for them.

*Values.* When I was a seminary student, I frequently heard professors and chapel speakers warn us about three great sins that put people out of the ministry: immorality, love of money and pride. (Today you would have to add plagiarism.) The warning is biblical. In Paul's first letter to Timothy, he had a good deal to say about money and the Christian life (6:6–10, 17–19), and in his second letter Paul told Timothy to maintain personal purity (2:22) and to avoid pride and the love of money (3:2).

Over the years I've changed my mind about wealth—not because I've received so much of it but because I think I've gotten a better understanding what Scripture has to say about it. I used to think that wealth was neutral and could be used either for good or evil, but I've concluded that wealth is intrinsically evil *until it is given to the Lord and sanctified by His blessing.*

Jesus called wealth "mammon," which is the Aramaic word for "riches, wealth." (The NIV translates it "Money," with a capital M.) In fact, He called it "the mammon of unrighteousness"

(Luke 16:9, 11, KJV; "worldly wealth," NIV) and saw wealth as a potential god that could capture our hearts and control our lives (Matt. 6:24; Luke 16:13). Paul classified the love of money ("filthy lucre," KJV) along with drunkenness and violence (1 Tim. 3:3; see Titus 1:7, 11), and Peter echoed his warnings (1 Pet. 5:2). People who trust their wealth but not God have made wealth their god, so that covetousness is really idolatry (Col. 3:5) and involves breaking three of the Ten Commandments—the first two and the last.

---

*It's not a sin to possess wealth, but it is a sin for wealth to possess us.*

---

Babies are born naked and poor, but God cares for them all during their nine months in their mother's womb, *and He can care for them for the rest of their lives if they will let Him.* Paul doesn't say it's wrong to be wealthy but that it's dangerous to "want to get rich" (1 Tim. 6:9), to focus your heart, mind and strength on that one dangerous goal. If we are faithful and God wants to bless us with wealth, He can do it and He can help us use it wisely. Abraham was a very wealthy man, and so was David; but wealth was their servant and not their master. "For the love of money is a root of all kinds of evil" (1 Tim. 6:10). That verse could be the epitaph for Lot (Gen. 13), Balaam (Num. 22–24), Achan (Joshua 7), Judas (Matt. 26:14–16), Demas (2 Tim. 4:9) and a host of other people who have made money their god.

God's ministers are admonished to instruct those who are "rich in this present world" to put their faith in God and not in riches, and to use their wealth to serve the Lord and not to please themselves (1 Tim. 6:17–19). You can be rich in this present world and yet poor in the next world, but you can also be poor in this world and rich in the next, and rich in this world and rich in the next! (Read 2 Cor. 6:10, Luke 12:13–21, 16:19–31 and 21:1–4.) It's not a sin to possess wealth, but it is a sin for wealth to possess us.

In these few pages we have not begun to lay hold of the spiritual principles of ministry Paul has shared with us, but you can take it from here. I urge my younger friends in the ministry to invest an hour or two a week with the pastoral epistles and some excellent commentaries, patiently digging out the treasures that are there. But don't stop with only studying them. Share them with your church family and seek to apply them in your own life. Pray that God will write them on your heart so that you will obey them instinctively and become a "good minister of Christ Jesus, nourished on the truths of the faith" (1 Tim. 4:6).

# 7

⧖

# Listening to the Holy Spirit

DURING the apostolic age God's servant Paul wrote letters to churches in seven different cities; and at the close of the apostolic age, the apostle John sent messages from Jesus Christ to churches in seven cities in Asia Minor. He commended two of the churches and warned the other five to repent (Rev. 2:5, 16, 21–22; 3:3, 19). When most believers study the Book of Revelation today, they usually take the traditional "prophetic view" of these seven letters and then move on to Revelation 4, totally ignoring what these epistles are saying to pastors and congregations today.

Vance Havner used to remind us that Christ's last words to the church were not Matthew 28:18–20, the so-called "Great Commission," but "Repent, or else"—and he was right. Five times in Revelation 2–3, the Lord tells churches to repent, and seven times He says to them and to us, "Whoever has ears, let them hear what the Spirit says to the churches" (Rev. 2:7, 11, 17, 29; 3:6, 13, 22). Note the plural—"churches." Not just the churches in Asia Minor but the churches in the world today.

I wonder how many ministers and church officers ask leaders in other churches, "What is the Spirit saying to you and your congregation?" Of course, some church leaders have no idea that the Spirit is speaking at all today, and they go on imitating other churches and drifting further and further from the will of God. Do leaders in denominations and other parachurch ministries share with one another what the Spirit is saying to them, or aren't they listening? Do they ever meet together to search the Scriptures, pray and seek the Spirit's leading? That appears to be what the Lord wants us to do.

---

*Both in my pastoral and parachurch ministries, I frequently asked people I respected, "What is the Lord saying to you these days?"*

---

Both in my pastoral and parachurch ministries, I frequently asked people I respected, "What is the Lord saying to you these days?" This question has often led to some heart-searching discussions and profitable times of prayer. I have asked staff members what the Lord was saying to them about our ministry, and their replies have greatly helped me, and I trust that I helped my fellow workers. To me, determining the will of God is something like assembling a jigsaw puzzle, *and I don't have all the pieces.* As my associates and I talk and pray together, each of us puts in a piece, and in God's time we see the whole picture.

I have a great fear of the people whom my younger friends call "the control freaks"—men and women who always know God's will and accept no suggestions and listen to no loving criticism. "Go my way or hit the highway" is their policy, and they can always find fawning flatterers who will salute and obey. They prefer security to integrity.

As for me, I want to follow the example of David who developed leaders (2 Sam. 23) and not the example of Rehoboam, who surrounded himself with cheerleaders (2 Chron. 10). The respected newspaper columnist Walter Lippmann said, "The final test of a leader is that he leaves behind him in other men the conviction and the will to carry on." You can't do that with cheerleaders.

Before John received the messages for the seven churches, he had an extraordinary vision of Christ walking in the midst of seven golden lampstands, a vision that was so overpowering that he fell at His feet as though he had been slain (Rev. 1:9–10). At the Last Supper John had rested his head on the bosom of Jesus as an intimate friend (John 13:25; 21:20), but now the sight of the glorified Priest-King so overwhelmed John that he fell before Jesus like a dead man. Why?

This event reminds us that *before we can worship and receive God's Word, we must by faith see the transcendent Savior and honor Him.* The prophet Daniel had a similar vision and wrote, "I had no strength left, my face turned deathly pale and I was helpless" (Dan. 10). Then God gave him the message to deliver to his people.

It's a basic principle of Christian worship that transcendence must precede immanence. As worshipers, we must first see Jesus "high and lifted up" (Isa. 6; John 12:39–41) before we lean on His breast as friends. Recognizing and acknowledging the greatness of God prepares the way for our experience of the grace of God. *Forgetting this principle has just about destroyed true worship in many churches.* Worship services now begin with "Hello, folks! We're glad you're here! Isn't it a beautiful day outside?" This is followed by the people in the congregation hugging or shaking hands and then singing some juvenile welcome chorus that re-peatedly says that God is with us (immanence).

But this approach is opposite of what the Word teaches. Our first obligation is to bow before the exalted Christ and recognize His glory and power (transcendence), because the majesty of Christ prepares us for the personal ministry of Christ in our lives (immanence). Only then can the God above us in glory be the God with us in our daily walk.

"Low thoughts of the Lord Jesus Christ are exceedingly mischievous to believers," said Charles Haddon Spurgeon, "If you sink in your estimate of Him, you shift everything else in the same proportion."[10] A.W. Tozer agrees with him. "The decline of the knowledge of the holy has brought on our troubles," he wrote. "A rediscovery of the majesty of God will go a long way toward curing them." He also said, "The essence of idolatry is the entertainment of thoughts about God that are unworthy of Him . . . .The first step down for any church is taken when it surrenders its high opinion of God."[11]

Alas, many professed Christians enthusiastically "worship" an imaginary God of their own invention and go home from a church service "feeling good" because they have been "spiritual." Ask the prophet Daniel and the apostle John how they felt after beholding the glorious, transcendent Savior!

Please note that Jesus was "in the middle of the lampstands," the place of honor and access (Rev. 1:13 NASB). The Book of Revelation has a dual emphasis: worship in heaven and warfare on earth. Churches on earth may put Jesus outside the door (3:20), but in heaven Jesus is the center of attraction and always belongs "in the midst," at the center. Later, John will see Him "standing at the center before the throne" (5:6; 7:17). During our Lord's ministry on earth, John had heard Jesus say, "For where two or three have gathered together in my name, I am there in their midst" (Matt. 18:20 NASB). In His death He was crucified "in the midst" between two malefactors (John 19:18), and in His resurrection He was "in the midst of the assembly" (Ps. 22:22 NASB; see Luke 24:36 and John 20:19, 26).

When it comes to the church's relationship to Jesus Christ, we must do on earth what the saints and angels do in heaven: ". . . so that in everything he might have the supremacy" (Col. 1:18).

---

*Where the Spirit is in control, Jesus is glorified.*

---

In Revelation 2 and 3, when Jesus speaks to each church, He begins with a statement from the description given of Him in Revelation 1:9–16. *The Holy Spirit was sent to glorify Christ, and when the Spirit speaks, He will not divorce the exalted Head of the church from the individual churches.* If the church body assembles to worship, the Head of that body must be honored and put in charge. Unfortunately, some of our churches are made up of people who think they are filled with the Spirit when they may be fooled by the spirits. They forget that Satan is an imitator who desperately wants to be worshiped (Matt. 4:8–11). Where Jesus is ignored, Satan is exalted. Where the Spirit is in control, Jesus is glorified.

But why does the Book of Revelation, a book of prophecy (Rev. 1:3; 22:7, 10, 18, 19), begin with an examination of seven local churches? The apostle Peter gives us the answer: "For it is time for judgment to begin with God's household" (1 Pet. 4:17). "Begin at my sanctuary," God told the six angels who were to execute His judgment in Jerusalem (Ezek. 9:1–6), and that has always been His policy.

God judges His own people first because it is our disobedience that has deprived the sinful world of a saving knowledge of Jesus Christ. If we believers were more faithful as light and salt (Matt. 5:13–16), there would be less darkness and decay in the world, and more people would know Jesus as their Lord and Savior. Because the Lord doesn't want anybody to perish but all to come to repentance, He is patient with *His own people* who ought to be getting out the gospel (2 Pet. 3:9). How much longer will He wait?

We could examine each of these seven churches in detail and learn much about what builds or destroys a ministry. However, I want to return to the emphasis in this book on *doors*, because Jesus speaks about doors to two of these churches. To the church in Philadelphia He said, "See, I have placed before you an open door that no one can shut" (Rev. 3:8). To the church in Laodicea, He said, "Here I am! I stand at the door and knock. If anyone hears my voice and opens the door, I will come in and eat with them, and they with me" (Rev. 3:20). An open door and a closed door—only this time it is not the unbelievers but *the believers* who have closed the door on the Lord!

The churches in Smyrna and Philadelphia received no criticism from the Lord, while the churches in Sardis and Laodicea received no commendation. The saints in Laodicea thought they were rich when they were actually poor (3:17), while the saints in Smyrna thought they were poor when they were actually rich (2:9). You can't evaluate a church on the basis of budgets, buildings and crowds. "The Lord does not look at the things human beings look at," God told Samuel. "People look at the outward appearance, but the Lord looks at the heart" (1 Sam. 16:7).

Let's visit first the "church of the open door" at the Asian city of Philadelphia ("love the brothers"). This city was established where three political regions met and several key roads intersected, because the primary purpose of the city was the spread

Greek culture. The city was called "the little Athens." In that strategic location the Lord planted a church for the purpose of spreading the message of the gospel of Jesus Christ. The Greeks and Romans saw Philadelphia as a "key city," but John saw Jesus Christ as the one who held the keys! He is the "key man." He had opened the door for the church to minister and promised to help them do the job.

It was my privilege to minister with *Back to the Bible* radio broadcast for almost ten years. For five of those years, I served together with its founder and Bible teacher, Theodore Epp. A modest man and a godly man, his only ambition was to spread God's Word, and he taught me a great deal about ministering by faith. Early in my ministry there, some of the stations and networks began changing their programming and moving from traditional Christian music, especially hymnody, to the "contemporary" sound. Some of them threatened to drop *Back to the Bible* if we didn't follow their example.

"What are we going to do?" I asked Mr. Epp one day as we discussed the matter. He reached for the Bible on his desk and said, "Let me show you something." He opened the Bible to Revelation 3:8 and read the verse to me: "See, I have placed before you an open door that no one can shut."

Leaving the Bible open, he said to me, "That's the promise God gave me when we began this ministry, and that promise still stands. Jesus holds the keys. When He opens a door, nobody can shut it, and when He shuts a door, we'd better not try to pry it open. Jesus is in charge, and we'll let Him do what He knows is best. Our responsibility is to obey."

Jesus opens and closes doors for those who have kept His Word and have not denied His name (Rev. 3:8). When our motive is to magnify the name of Jesus, and our message is the Word of the Lord, God will direct as He sees fit. We may not always understand His plan (remember Acts 16:6–10?), but we know He has one.

The believers in the church in Philadelphia had little strength *and they admitted it*, and this qualified them to draw on the unfailing strength of the Lord. (The phrase "little strength" can also mean "small in number.") But the people in the church of Laodicea didn't know their poverty and pitiable plight, so the Lord couldn't help them. Satan was opposing the ministry of the church in Philadelphia (3:9), but Satan had already captured the church in Laodicea, and the church didn't realize it. Jesus was outside the door of the church, trying to get in.

What kept the church in Philadelphia faithful and fruitful, in spite of their small number and small strength? The people glorified Jesus Christ, proclaimed and obeyed God's Word, depended on God's strength and looked forward to the coming of Jesus. "I am coming soon. Hold on to what you have, so that no one will take your crown" (3:11).

---

*The return of Jesus isn't discussed much in the church fellowship, only at the funeral home or the cemetery.*

---

I remember back when several churches banded together in a city for week-long conferences on prophecy, but you rarely see this today. Church members are so comfortable in this present evil age that they talk about heaven and Christ's coming only when somebody is found to have a life-threatening disease or somebody dies. The return of Jesus isn't discussed much in the church fellowship, only at the funeral home or the cemetery.

One day the door in heaven will be opened and, like the apostle John, God's people will be "called up" to the throne room of the Almighty (Rev. 4:1; 1 Thess. 4:13–18). Then we will appear at the judgment seat of Christ and discover whether or not we have been negligent and forfeited our crowns or been faithful and won His rewards.

Eight times in the Book of Revelation, the apostle John mentions a group of people called "the inhabitants of the earth" (6:10; 8:13; 10:10; 13:8, 12, 14; 17:2, 8). This phrase means much more than "people living on the earth." It refers to "people living *for* the world and depending only on the world for their existence." Unlike God's people, whose names are written in heaven (Luke 10:20), these are unsaved people whose names are not written in God's book of life (Rev. 17:8). They have left God out of their lives and are living on substitutes provided by the world system.

Even in apostolic times, some of these people had gotten into local churches and tried to divert them from the truth, and sometimes they were successful (Phil. 3:17–21; 2 Pet. 2:1–3; 1 John 2:18–29). *This is how faithful churches become infected and polluted by the world and false doctrine, and finally become conformed to the world.* When spiritual leaders relax their oversight, then the "yeast" enters the loaf (1 Cor. 5:5–8; Gal. 5:9) and silently grows until the loaf becomes "puffed up." This is a metaphor for the arrogance of those who no longer magnify Jesus Christ (1 Cor. 4:6, 18, 19; 5:2; 8:1; Col. 2:18).

John describes these "inhabitants of the earth" as religious people, *but they worshiped antichrist and not Christ* (Rev. 13:8, 12, 14). They were intoxicated with the worldly harlot Babylon (17:1–18) and not devoted to the heavenly bride and the holy city of God (Rev. 19:1–8; 21:1–27). They rejected the ministry of God's true prophets (11:1–12) and therefore were destined for judgment (6:10; 8:13). The word "antichrist" means both "against Christ" (Satan the lion) and "instead of Christ" (Satan the serpent, the counterfeiter).

The church in Laodicea had been taken over by the world and therefore had the values and appetites of the world. Instead of being an incarnation of the Lord, they existed by imitation of the world system. The church went through the motions of ministry but was lukewarm in its motivation.

The Christian life knows only three "temperatures": the burning heart (Luke 24:32), the lukewarm heart (Rev. 3:15) and the cold heart (Matt. 24:12). Paul admonished Timothy, "I remind you to fan into flame the gift of God which is in you" (2 Tim. 1:6), and he wrote to the assemblies in Rome, "Never be lacking in zeal, but keep your spiritual fervor, serving the Lord" (Rom. 12:11). Literally he says "in spirit—burning, boiling hot."

The church in Laodicea thought it was successful, but in the eyes of Jesus, it was a dismal failure. "The church was in a rich city," wrote A.T. Robertson, "and was rich in pride and conceit, but poor in grace and ignorant of its spiritual poverty."[12]

A cup of hot liquid doesn't get lukewarm in an instant; it takes time for the temperature gradually to fall to the point where nobody will drink it. Churches don't suddenly lose their spiritual fervor; it's a gradual decline from the founding generation to the third or fourth generation, when most churches and parachurch ministries begin to decline (see Judges 2:6ff). "When churches get into the condition of half-hearted faith," said Charles Spurgeon, "tolerating the gospel, but having a sweet tooth for error, they do far more mischief to their age than downright heretics."[13] If you had asked the believers at Laodicea, "How shall we pray for your church?" they would have replied, "Oh, we don't need anything!" They were independent and self-sufficient. Campbell Morgan described the Laodicean church as "an influential church without influence."[14] In that same message he said, "The most difficult congregation in the world to which to preach the gospel is the congregation that regularly listens to it and refuses to obey it."[15]

This kind of church may be featured in leading religious magazines and even in the secular press, but its "ministry" makes little or no lasting impact on the unconverted world we are supposed to reach. The late president of Moody Bible Institute, Dr. William Culbertson, said it perfectly: "A surfeited, cynical, yet fearful world looks at all our machinery and all our bricks and mortar, and all our gadgets and devices, and is utterly unimpressed."[16]

It's worth noting that Paul mentioned the Laodicean church four times in his letter to the Colossians. He told the Colossian saints that he was struggling in prayer for them and also for the Laodicean church (Col. 2:1), and that Epaphras—probably the founding pastor of the Colossian church (1:7)—was "wrestling in prayer" for the Laodicean saints (4:13). After sending greetings from Luke and Demas, Paul greeted some believers at Laodicea and commanded that the Colossian epistle be read in their assembly. Also, the letter Paul had sent to Laodicea should be read by the Colossian church (Col. 4:14–16).

---

*The important question in ministry isn't what we think of the church or even what the congregation or the public thinks.*

---

Once again we see the ministry of the Word of God and prayer joined together for the building of the church (Acts 6:4). Yet, in spite of the fervent prayers of two godly men and the inspired truth of Paul's epistle to the Colossians, the believers at Laodicea failed miserably and created such a worldly atmosphere in their assembly that Jesus had to leave the church. Our Lord used a vivid and certainly unexpected image when He said, "I am about to spit you out of my mouth" (Rev. 3:16). It's as though He were saying, "I'm disgusted! Your church makes me sick!" After all, the important question in ministry isn't what we think of the church or even what the congregation or the public thinks, but what the Lord thinks; and the only way we can determine that is by searching the Scriptures and waiting on the Lord in prayer. "Whoever has ears, let them hear what the Spirit says to the churches."

But there is a positive side to our Lord's examination and evaluation of these seven churches. Like any good physician, He wants to encourage the healthy and help the unhealthy. His indictment is for the purpose of improvement; He wants to cure, not condemn. The evidences of this are obvious.

To begin with, *He speaks to the churches and calls them to listen.* He didn't abandon them to their own destructive ways—although with five of them, He may have had good reason to do so—but instead He showed them the x-rays and told them the truth. Knowing their hearts as He did, He could have turned His back on them and spoken to them no more. The silence of God is greater judgment than the thunder and lightning of His wrath. "For if you remain silent, I will be like those who go down to the pit" (Ps. 28:1).

*He calls them churches—"called out ones."* When you consider the errors and sinful disobedience that He found in five of the churches, do they really qualify as "churches"? Most of the believers in Sardis had soiled their clothes (Rev. 3:4), the believers in Pergamum were involved in idolatry and immorality (2:14), and the church at Thyatira was tolerating the influence of an immoral woman and studying "the deep secrets of Satan" (2:20–21, 24). How carnal can a church become and still call itself a church?

*He affirms His love for them* (3:9, 19). Christ's words in Revelation 2 and 3 are good examples of "speaking the truth in love" (Eph. 4:15): "Those whom I love I rebuke and discipline" (3:19, and see Heb. 12:5–6 and Prov. 3:11–12). "Christ loved the church" and died for the church, and He longs to minister cleansing to those congregations that desperately need it (Eph. 5:25–27). Like a good physician, He may hurt us but He will never harm us. He knows whether or not a church loves Him (2:4, 19), and His rebukes and disciplines are evidences of His love (3:19). The Lord disciplined the church in Corinth (1 Cor. 11:30–32) and gave warning of possible discipline to the churches in Ephesus (2:4–5), Pergamum (2:16), Thyatira (2:21–23), Sardis (3:3) and Laodicea (3:19).

Yes, "love covers a multitude of sins" (1 Pet. 4:8; Prov. 10:12), which means we don't go around talking about somebody's sins; but love can never condone sin. Parents love their children too much to allow them to go their own sinful way, and God's love for us is greater than that of any earthly parent. The church that compromises and gives in to unbiblical practices to achieve "peace at any price" is disobeying God's Word. "But the wisdom that comes from heaven is first of all pure; then peace-loving, considerate, submissive . . ." (James 3:17). Purity comes before peace because, in the spiritual life, purity is the first step toward peace (Isa. 32:17).

*He doesn't command the faithful to abandon the churches.* Instead, He commands the sinners to repent and stop sinning, and He commands the godly remnant in the church to hold fast to what they have and keep being faithful (2:4–5, 14–15, 24–25; 3:1–5, 18–20). The Bible does teach personal separation from sin (1 Cor. 5:9–13; 2 Cor. 6:14–7:1) and from doctrinal error (Rom. 16:17–19; 1 Tim. 4; 1 John 2:18–29). In these letters we get the impression that the Lord wants the faithful ones to remain and be a powerful spiritual influence as they pray and serve. Should God judge the church and remove the lampstand (Rev. 2:9), or "spit them out" (3:16), we assume that the faithful saints would be free to leave and become part of a godly fellowship. God's encouragements and God's warnings both come from His heart of love.

*He patiently calls to the church, knocks on the door and waits.* In his expanded translation of the New Testament, Kenneth Wuest brings out some of the nuances of Rev. 3:20: "Consider this. I have taken my stand at the door and am politely knocking. If anyone hears my voice and opens the door, I will come in to him, and I will dine with him and he himself will dine with me."[17]

There is something sad to see: Jesus taking a stand outside His church for which He died. There is something gracious to hear: His repeated knocks on the door and His voice repeatedly calling to us. He hasn't given up on us! There is something decisive to do: open the door and let Him come in and take control. Finally, there is something wonderful to enjoy: enriching fellowship with the Lord. *He comes in as a guest but then becomes the Host, the Master!* The sooner that happens the better off the church will be.

---

*Let's confess the sins that have kept us from pleasing Him, repent and turn from them. "So be earnest and repent" is His command (3:19).*

---

*He is willing to begin with only one person.* Our Lord doesn't ask for a quorum to gather and give Him a majority vote. There is nothing to discuss but time to act, and we must not lose the opportunity. I suggest you read Song of Solomon 5:2–8 and meditate on this record of a similar situation involving the Lord and one person, in this case, His beloved. She was too comfortable to get up and open the door, and when she finally decided to act, He had gone. If one believer in the church will respond to the Lord's call, it could mean the beginning of new life in the church. Everywhere in the Book of Revelation, Jesus Christ is honored *except in 3:20.* There He is humiliated, ignored and kept outside the door.

If we want to be among those who welcome Him back into His church, what must we do? I suggest that first we read Revelation 1:9–18, meditate on it and ask the Spirit to open the eyes of our hearts to see Jesus Christ in His glory (Eph. 1:15–23). Then let's read Revelation 2–3, especially noting what Jesus said to the saints in Ephesus and Laodicea, and accept the diagnosis He presents us. Let's confess the sins that have kept us from pleasing Him, repent and turn from them. "So be earnest and repent" is His command (3:19).

Repentance isn't just being sorry for our sins; it's being sorry enough to stop sinning. Then let's accept His invitation to dinner and spend time feeding on His Word as He instructs us by His Spirit. If we are sincere, He will come into our lives in a fresh way and work in us and through us to bring new blessing to others.

When God wanted to save the Jewish nation during a famine, He got hold of one person—Joseph. When He wanted to deliver His people from bondage, He called one man—Moses. It was because of the prayers and dedication of one woman—Hannah—that new spiritual life came to Israel in the birth of Samuel, and her New Testament counterpart was Mary, the mother of Jesus, the Savior of the world. One courageous woman, Esther, rescued Israel from annihilation.

God speaks in Ezekiel 22:30: "I looked for someone among them who would build up the wall and stand before me in the gap on behalf of the land so I would not have to destroy it, but I found no one." Are you the "someone" God is searching for?

The door of the church may be closed to Jesus, but you and I can personally open the door and have a new meeting with Him that could eventually transform others.

I'm closing this book with the same statement that opened it: "The history of the church is the sad record of the conflict between open doors and closed minds."

What will you do about it?

*I will venture to prophesy that the less help she [the church] seeks from the world, and the more she leans upon God, the brighter will her future be.*

Charles Haddon Spurgeon[18]

# Endnotes

1. A.W. Tozer, *The Tozer Pulpit*, vol. 2 (Camp Hill, PA: Christian Publications, 1994), 12.

2. This statement must not be construed to mean that it's wrong for ministries to have buildings. Paul moved into a private home next to the synagogue in Corinth (Acts 18:7), rented a schoolroom in Ephesus (Acts 19:9–10) and hired a house for his ministry in Rome (Acts 28:30-31). However, it is wrong to take money that ought to be invested in people and ministry, and waste it on unnecessary real estate.

3. Watchman Nee, *The Joyful Heart* (Carol Stream, IL: Tyndale House, 1978), August 15.

4. Charles H. Spurgeon, *Metropolitan Tabernacle Pulpit*, vol. 28 (London: Passmore and Alabaster, 1895), 152.

5. Os Guinness, *Dining With the Devil* (Ada, MI: Baker, 1993), 21.

6. Francis Schaeffer, *The Church Before the Watching World* (Downers Grove, IL: InterVarsity, 1971), 12.

7.   George Duffield, Jr., "Stand Up, Stand Up for Jesus" (hymn), 1858, public domain.

8.   G.F. Barbour, *Life of Alexander Whyte, D.D.* (London: Hodder and Stoughton, 1923), 282.

9.   Eric Hoffer, *Reflections on the Human Condition* (New York: HarperCollins, 1973), 22.

10.  Charles H. Spurgeon, *Metropolitan Tabernacle Pulpit*, vol. 18 (London: Passmore and Alabaster, 1895), 1.

11.  A.W. Tozer, *The Knowledge of the Holy* (New York: HarperCollins, 1961), 7, 11–12.

12.  A.T. Robertson, *Word Pictures in the New Testament*, vol. 6 (Nashville: Broadman Press, 1930), 322.

13.  Charles H. Spurgeon, *Metropolitan Tabernacle Pulpit*, vol. 20 (London: Passmore and Alabaster, 1895), 424.

14.  G. Campbell Morgan, *Westminster Pulpit*, vol. 6 (London: Pickering and Inglis, n.d.,), 24.

15.  Ibid., 38.

16.  Dr. William Culbertson, *The Faith Once Delivered* (Chicago: Moody Press, 1972), 57.

17.  Kenneth Wuest, *The New Testament: An Expanded Translation* (Grand Rapids, MI: Eerdmans, 1961).

18.  Charles H. Spurgeon, *Metropolitan Tabernacle Pulpit*, vol. 63 (London: Passmore and Alabaster, 1895), 125.

This book was produced by CLC Publications. We hope it has been life-changing and has given you a fresh experience of God through the work of the Holy Spirit. CLC Publications is an outreach of CLC Ministries International, a global literature mission with work in over fifty countries. If you would like to know more about us or are interested in opportunities to serve with a faith mission, we invite you to contact us at:

CLC Ministries International
PO Box 1449
Fort Washington, PA 19034

*Phone:* 215-542-1242
*E-mail:* orders@clcpublications.com
*Website:* www.clcpublications.com

## DO YOU LOVE GOOD CHRISTIAN BOOKS?
*Do you have a heart for worldwide missions?*

You can receive a FREE subscription to
CLC's newsletter on global literature missions
*Order by e-mail at:*

**clcworld@clcusa.org**

*Or fill in the coupon below and mail to:*

**PO Box 1449
Fort Washington, PA 19034**

---

### FREE *CLC WORLD* SUBSCRIPTION!

Name: _____

Address:_____

_____

Phone: _____ E-mail:_____

# READ THE REMARKABLE STORY OF
*the founding of*
## CLC International

*Leap of Faith*

*"Any who doubt that Elijah's God still lives ought to read of the money supplied when needed, the stores and houses provided, and the appearance of personnel in answer to prayer."* —Moody Monthly

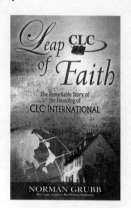

Is it possible that the printing press, the editor's desk, the Christian bookstore and the mail order department can glow with the fast-moving drama of an "Acts of the Apostles"?

Find the answer as you are carried from two people in an upstairs bookroom to a worldwide chain of Christian bookcenters multiplied by nothing but a "shoestring" of faith and by committed, though unlikely, lives.

**Other Warren Wiersbe Titles**
**Published by CLC Publications**

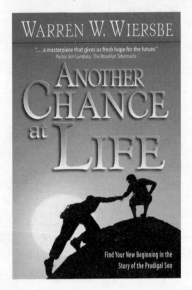

*ANOTHER CHANCE AT LIFE*

Warren W. Wiersbe

**When you've really blown it . . .**
**. . . is there any way out of the mess?**

In his unique depiction of the prodigal son, Warren Wiersbe examines the cast of characters from this well-known story and draws lessons from each individual. Find yourself in the wasteful son, or perhaps in the spiteful brother, and recognize afresh the One who can forgive every sin—our merciful Father.

If you've left the path of grace and think you've gone too far, or if you simply need a reminder of God's mercy and love, this book holds a welcome dose of encouragement. Your Father is waiting to receive you, ready to give you *another chance at life.*

*ISBN-10: 0-87508-996-8*
*ISBN-13: 978-0-87508-996-6*

*EXPERT LIFEMANSHIP*

Warren Wiersbe and Ken Jenkiins

### What do we do with life?

Sometimes life's crises, or even its predictability, can derail us from the path of God's purpose. He intends, however, that we live to the full. Learning to wait on Him for His overcoming strength will enable us to "rise up with wings as eagles, run and not be weary, walk and not faint."

This grand theme is explored in the words of Warren Wiersbe, punctuated by the stunning nature photography of Ken Jenkins. What is created is an appealing invitation to get a new perspective on your existence in this world—and maybe change your life.

Full color photos and text included.

*Coffee Table Book  ISBN: 978-0-87508-988-1*

## Other Warren Wiersbe Titles
## Published by CLC Publications

*LET'S GO!*

*Warren W. Wiersbe*

### The Epistle to the Hebrews for Twenty-first-Century Christians

Does the book of Hebrews seem daunting to you? Let Warren Wiersbe unfold principles from this timeless letter which can turn quitters into conquerors and produce a vibrant, productive life.

As you study the book of Hebrews along with Wiersbe, you will grow in your walk with the Lord, mature in your faith and discover the calling He has for you. Get ready to go in (Heb. 1–4), go on (Heb. 5–6), go up (Heb. 7–10) and go out (Heb. 11–13)!

*ISBN 13: 978-1-936143-07-8*

*TOO SOON TO QUIT!*

*Warren W. Wiersbe*

**Ready to quit?**
**You're not the only one.**
**Flip through the pages of Scripture—you're in good company.**

Warren Wiersbe unfolds the stories of fifteen Bible characters who struggled just like you—people we now consider high-endurance saints, such as

- Abraham, who discovered that outlook determines outcome;
- Job, who learned to live on promises, not explanations;
- Ruth, who proved that decision and determination influence destiny;
- Habakkuk, who faced the facts, but kept walking by faith;
- Paul, who found that if you keep growing you can keep going.

With the skill of a master storyteller, Wiersbe draws from the pages of God's Word to give us the strength to survive—and thrive—when the road gets rocky and the pathway steep. Get your second wind from these faithful lives as you learn that it's too soon to quit!

*ISBN 13: 978-1-936143-00-9*